✦ ✦ ✦

WEIGHT TRAINING

for

MARTIAL ARTS

✦ ✦ ✦

Prior to beginning any exercise program, you must consult with your physician. You must also consult your physician before increasing the intensity of your training. The information in this book is intended for healthy individuals. Any application of the recommended material in this book is at the sole risk of the reader, and at the reader's discretion. Responsibility of any injuries or other adverse effects resulting from the application of any of the information provided within this book is expressly disclaimed.

Published by Price World Publishing
3971 Hoover Rd. Suite 77
Columbus, OH 43123-2839
www.PriceWorldPublishing.com

Cover Design by Russell Marleau
Layout Design by Merwin Loquias
Editing by Sangeeta Sinha
Photographs by Thomas Zamiar
Modeling by Katalin Rodriguez-Ogren and David Ogren
Printing by Cushing-Malloy, Inc.

ISBN: 978-1-932549-713
eBook ISBN: 978-1-619843-585

Printed in the United States of America
10 9 8 7 6 5 4 3 2 1

For information about discounts for bulk purchases, please contact info@priceworldpublishing.com.

WEIGHT TRAINING

for

MARTIAL ARTS

The Ultimate Guide

KATALIN RODRIGUEZ-OGREN

PW

PRICE WORLD
PUBLISHING

ACKNOWLEDGMENTS

I was able to write this book because of so many people.

First, thank you mom, The Almighty Isis, for signing me up for my first karate class.

Thank you also to:

My husband, Dave, for granting me the time to write.

My father, Thomas Zamiar, for continued support & every picture you have ever taken.

My friend, Jennifer Imig, for taking on so many of my responsibilities at POW! MMA & Fitness.

My friend, Bernie Lecocq, for being my reliable sounding board.

My friend, Paul Reavlin, Owner of Revgear for supporting all my educational programs.

My favorite Editors, Doug Jeffrey, Dave Cater & Bob Young for publishing my articles since 1997.

Move quickly.
Sound, calm mind.
Be light in body.
Have a clever mind.
Master the basics.
- Gogen Yamaguchi, Five Secrets of Japanese Goju Ryu

Outside of my family, the martial arts have shaped many aspects of my character. It has given back to me tenfold. To this day, I use many of the first lessons I ever learned in martial arts. My mother enrolled me in my first martial arts program when I was 9 years old. I studied Okinawan Karate (Goju Ryu). Before this, I was committed to classical ballet at The Ruth Page School of Ballet in Chicago. Since the age of 4, my parents watched over my dance training with hopes that I would become a ballerina. Looking back, I realize now that Goju Ryu Karate was the antithesis of ballet. However, it provided an excellent foundation for a future martial artist. Ballet offered the yin, and I was about to embark on learning the yang. My instructor used to call me Yamaguchi. He was not referring to the Olympic ice skater (Kristi Yamaguchi), but to Gogen Yamaguchi, the barely 5-foot karate master. He drew this comparison because I was fixated with the basics. My classical ballet training emphasized that true art unfolds from your barre technique. So I applied the same work ethic to the martial arts and rarely complained about practicing basic punches, kicks and stances (which in essence was the equivalent to barre work).

The words written above by Yamaguchi are a great summary of how to get started in anything. This book will hopefully inspire you to quickly embrace the need to add purposeful strength training into your martial arts program. Make sound decisions in how to go about adding exercises with a calm mind. Approach each workout routine with a solid grasp of the exercises you have chosen. Be clever in integrating them into your martial arts training routine while keeping the big picture in mind – a stronger and healthier body. And lastly, master the basics of the strength training exercises dispersed throughout this book, which will lead to an enjoyable and pain-free martial athletic career.

.

~ **Katalin Rodriguez-Ogren** ~

CONTENTS

Introduction 13

Part I: What is a Strong Body? 19

    The Modern Martial Artist 20

    What is Strength Training? 21

    How Does Strength Training Help You Lose Weight? 22

    Importance of Strengthening Connective Tissue 23

    Developing Power and Strength 24

    Ballistic Exercises 25

    Plyometric Exercises 26

    Strengthening Your Joints 27

    Bodyweight Training for the Martial Athlete 29

    Does Strength Training Make You Better at Martial Arts? 32

    Flexibility Training Enhances Strength 34

        Static Flexibility 34

        Dynamic Flexibility 35

        Dynamic Flexibility is not the Same as Ballistic Flexibility ... 36

        Assessing Flexibility 37

        Are Stretching Devices Valuable? 38

Part II: Getting Started 39

    Use Your Discipline Nature to Find Time to Strength Train 40

    5 Questions to Ask Before Getting Started 40

    The Most Important Part of Warming Up 43

    What is the best way to warm up? 43

    Importance of Breathing in All Training 46

    Will Meditation Help Me Learn to Breath Better? 47

Part III: Exercises 49

    Bodyweight Exercises 51

    The BOSU Balance Trainer 55

Core and Abs 61

Dumbbell Exercises 71

Dynamic Flexibility Exercises 79

Plyometrics 83

Suspension Strap Training 87

Cable Machines 95

KettleBells 113

Weight Machines 127

Part IV: Program Design 135

Introduction 136

Designing a Program is Mastering Change 136

Recapping Strength Training 137

Does a Fitness Professional Need to
Design Your Strength Training Program? 138

The Principles of Training 140

    Overload Principle 140

    Progression Principle 141

    Adaptation Principle 141

    Specificity Principle 142

    Recovery Principle 142

    Reversibility Principle 143

How Should I Format My Program? 143

    Format Type 1: Intervals 144

    Format Type 2: Counted Repetitions and Sets 146

The Big Picture - Structuring Your Programs Over
the Course of a Year 146

Types of Periodization 148

    Linear Periodization 148

    Concurrent Periodization 148

Age Matters, Do Not Fool Yourself 150

DEFINING PHASES, CYCLES and DAILY GOALS 153

    TBS (including Flexible Mobility and Core) 153

    Hypertrophy (with Flexible Mobility and Core) 154

Absolute Strength or One-Rep-Max
(with Flexible Mobility and Core) 155

Power (and Flexible Mobility and Core) 155

Muscular Endurance (with Flexible Mobility and Core).................. 155

Summarizing Program Design.. 157

Part V: Programs 163

Author Bio.. 187

Bibliography 188

INTRODUCTION

*W*eight Training for Martial Arts: The Ultimate Guide is the perfect book for any person who wants to lengthen their martial arts practice, and improve their overall strength and functional skill sets for martial arts. The exercises in this book are geared towards all types of martial artists. It will provide innovative strength training techniques for the overall enhancement of martial arts skills.

The traditional martial arts community has only recently embraced the concepts of strength training. The popularity of kickboxing-fitness classes in the 1990s, the induction of Tae Kwon Do into the Olympics in 2000, and the growth of the sport of Mixed Martial Arts (MMA) in the past 10 years have all positively influenced the martial arts community. As I wrote each section of this book, I found it challenging to choose only a handful of exercises because there are many useful training methods that complement the martial arts. This book will give you athletic strength training concepts that will improve your overall martial arts skills. You will also learn sport-specific exercises that are applicable to improving functional strength for all martial arts techniques. As you complete this book, you will find many ways to prevent injuries that may occur as a result of your martial arts practice, and therefore, lengthen your years in the martial arts.

As you begin reading each section, understand first that although you are called a martial "artist," I consider you an athlete. Punching, kicking, blocking, clinch-work, forms and even throwing all require the same fundamental athletic capabilities as boxers, tennis players and even football players. All of our movements require speed, power, control, strength, flexibility, endurance and good underlying cardiovascular fitness. You can integrate these exercises into your existing routine or utilize the "Programs" in Part V of this book to completely change your training program. Whichever type of program you choose, enhancing comprehensive strength must be addressed from a musculoskeletal point of view.

The martial arts community has been playing a bit of catch up over the past decade. In general, martial artists have been slow to use the athletic sciences as a tool for improving their training. Therefore, each section of this book summarizes and highlights key information you should know about strength training. This knowledge will lead to a more productive training experience in the martial arts. Beyond the accessibility of the education provided in each chapter, you will be given practical application, exercises, programs and dynamic drills you can try today! For example, you can look forward to increasing the speed of your strikes or eliminating back pain that occurs after forms training. The various strength programs and exercises given in this book are easy to follow and offer several options for all types of martial artists.

As you read each section, you will notice I use "artist" and "athlete" interchangeably. Although they have their own unique definitions, I do not believe you can be a martial artist today, without having an athletic perspective on training. With that being said, I hope you end up integrating many of the exercises included in this book to elevate your training while concurrently improving your overall fitness level and technical performance. As a modern day martial arts practitioner, your training program must include programming aspects that develop power, explosivity, muscular endurance and strength, dynamic flexibility and joint stability.

MARTIAL ATHLETICS ™ — THE EMERGING MODERN DAY PRACTITIONER

You are a member of the diverse martial arts community who understands that each style has evolved over hundreds of years. Each martial art offers a different experience. The origins and emphasis of each art can offer a student either an internal or an external lesson. Others give you throws verse kicking skills, and some art forms focus on reality combat verse katas. All these variances within the martial arts have always made me believe that there is a martial art suitable for everyone in the world.

Since the martial arts community is compromised of individual school owners and not supported by universities or collegiate programs, it has been hard to spread the evolving education in the exercise sciences. Individual school owners have only recently become highly receptive to the importance of strength training, the value of injury prevention and concepts like periodization and interval training. The information has become far more accessible and visible in the past 5 years to the school owner and their student, even though many of the concepts presented throughout this book first emerged 15-20 years ago.

Regardless of these variances amongst the martial arts community, athletic and strength training concepts can be tailored to the forms competitor, the MMA fighter, the devoted traditionalist and the tai chi follower. As you learn new strengthening exercises, you can insert them into your current practice or design a completely new training program that focuses on strengthening your body comprehensively for your martial art. I have included numerous strengthening programs at the end of the book that will help prevent injuries and lengthen your practice of martial arts. Enjoy each section of this book and thank you for having an interest in my lifelong endeavors in the martial arts.

WHEN I REALIZED I WAS AS MUCH ATHLETE AS I WAS ARTIST

It was in 1996 that I recognized the personal importance of yoga, weight training, plyometrics, injury prevention and interval work. Since then, all of these elements have been part of my martial arts training regiment. It was at this time that I began using the term martial athletics™. I decided I wanted to create strength training programs for martial artists. Regardless of an individual's style, each training program was designed to enhance overall athleticism, offer injury prevention and provide longevity in the martial arts. So I began to refer to myself as a martial athlete and not a martial artist. The transition from artist to athlete was also driven by the desire to make mainstream exercisers consider martial arts as a form of fitness that was better than cardio machines and basic weight training. The trick was to create workout routines that looked fun, while showcasing the best techniques of the martial arts. I focused on the athletic nature of punches, stances and kicks. I also wanted the athletic foundation of tae kwon do, judo, kung fu, karate, and jeet kun do to be better recognized, and viewed as completely appropriate for the adult market. So I stripped away some of the intimidating components and characteristics that prevented many adults from thinking that martial arts was just for kids. By restructuring the way in which a karate class looked, I was able to attract a new demographic. In essence, I gave traditional martial arts classes an athletic facelift.

This new martial arts package lured the adult market into practicing martial arts. I sold martial arts as a workout option by highlighting its fitness value. I counted on the raw gratification and fitness challenge of the basic punches and kicks. The next goal was to convince a potential customer that he or she could replace their health club membership with one to a martial arts school.

By 1997, I was teaching classes and workshops that combined martial arts along with cross training. My classes were comprised of high-energy martial arts drills that were formatted into intervals with weight lifting exercises, plyometrics and even dynamic flexibility. I was creating a new breed of martial art student. They were open-minded, fitness driven, motivated and eager for the most valuable lessons traditional martial arts had to offer. I taught and wrote programming for classes like cardio-kickboxing, heavy bag training, kickfit, stance strengthening routines and even MMA circuit workouts.

My first article was published in January of 1997. My first editor, Dave Cater, at *Inside Kung Fu Magazine* published "Building the Injury-Free Athlete." From there, I wrote a monthly column in *Martial Arts Training Magazine*, called *Peak Performance* that focused on the same topics covered in this book. In 1998-2009, I was able to expand on these topics and began writing regular features that were 4-12 pages in length dissecting strength training and the exercise sciences. My favorite articles were called *8 Week Strength Training Programs for Martial Artists, Adding Resistance Training to the Martial Art School and Cross-Training for the Martial Artis*t. My articles were published in national publications like *Martial Arts Legends Magazine, Black Belt, Karate Illustrated, Combat Sports, Ultimate Grappling* and many others.

The martial arts magazines recognized the need to spread the gospel of strength and cross training for martial artists. However, the key was to do it without infringing on the traditionalist's way of training. I continued to write articles that offered a way to cross-train as a complement to traditional practice. My articles accomplished this by promoting the importance of injury prevention. I catered to the desire of every martial artist, to lengthen his or her practice. I was lucky to have great editors that believed in the need to expose the traditionalists to new training concepts. In fact, these magazines were a little ahead of their time and there was a lot of resistance by school owners initially to make changes to class structures that existed for decades. But once the *Tae-Bo* and cardio-kickboxing craze emerged, more school owners and head instructors recognized the profitability of integrating fitness-driven formats into their curriculum.

Momentum was building as more magazines regularly added features and columns about exercises to improve martial arts skills. This included forms, sparring and weapons practice with all types of strength training exercises. Additional merit was given to this evolution when companies like Revgear Sports (www.revgear.com) added fitness programs and education to their catalogs. The growing interest in fitness-driven programming for the martial artist gave Revgear Sports the confidence to launch additional programs and products that brought comprehensive athletic programming to the traditional martial arts school. Without this commitment, the infusion of resistance band training to the martial arts school may have taken even longer. Martial arts schools eventually hungered for new concepts like martial athletics[TM], fitness-based kicking classes, interval training and competition form programs (i.e. XMA). These types of modern martial arts programs expanded the demographic, increased customer retention and diversified the public's perception of traditional martial arts.

PART I

WHAT IS A STRONG BODY?

*"Adding strength training to your routine
will lead to the pursuit of improving overall strength,
martial arts skills and health."*

THE MODERN MARTIAL ARTIST

We all wish we could turn back the clock. And believe it or not, there are many things that we can do to slow down the aging process or regain a younger sense of ourselves. Strength training will increase your lean body mass and keep you feeling younger and healthier. The past few decades have produced unanimous consensus that strength training should be part of every adult's life, no matter your age.

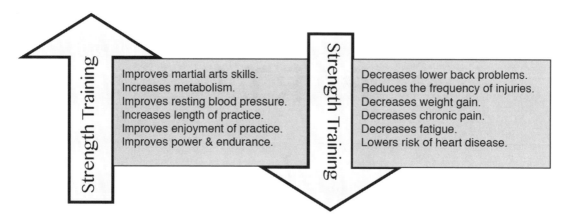

Strength Training

Improves martial arts skills.
Increases metabolism.
Improves resting blood pressure.
Increases length of practice.
Improves enjoyment of practice.
Improves power & endurance.

Strength Training

Decreases lower back problems.
Reduces the frequency of injuries.
Decreases weight gain.
Decreases chronic pain.
Decreases fatigue.
Lowers risk of heart disease.

Five Reasons for Strength Training

1. Without strength training, you may lose up to 3-10 pounds of muscle every decade of your life (this depends ultimately on your ideal body weight).
2. Muscle is comprised of highly active tissue, which is constantly breaking down and rebuilding itself. Strength training keeps your muscle tissue active. Without strength training, your metabolic rate will decrease.
3. Strength training has a positive effect on blood pressure. Regular exercise that includes strength training can lower your resting blood pressure.
4. Strength training can reduce and even prevent lower back problems.
5. Strength training can reduce joint pain, osteoporosis and arthritic symptoms.

WHAT IS STRENGTH TRAINING?

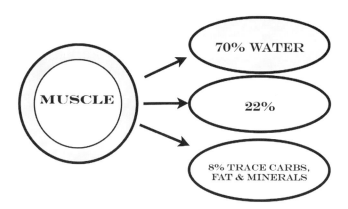

Strength training of the skeletal muscle involves performing exercises that place a load or resistance on the muscle. This effort forces the muscle to adapt. The adaptation in essence leads to the muscle tissue gaining strength and size. Muscle tissue is a highly adaptable tissue. It is comprised of mostly water, protein and a combination of trace carbohydrates, fat and minerals. The exercises you choose must force adaptation. You will learn that this can be accomplished by using free weights, cable machines, plated loaded machines, kettlebells, resistance tubing, sandbag, tires and even body weight. Whichever exercises you choose to use, you must regularly apply resistance to the muscle(s) involved in order for them to gain strength.

Strength training can be viewed as a supply and demand system. You want to increase the size of your muscles. You supply the body with continued and consistent resistance (i.e. a regular routine of weight lifting and protein of course), which stimulates muscle development and the body delivers by meeting the demand with a fortified production of muscle cells. On a cellular level, strength training (along with sufficient protein) changes the muscular structure and enhances the communication between the muscles and the nerves in the body. The hypertrophy that occurs from strength training, which refers simply to the growth of the muscle, is a highly desirable affect of strength training.

It was once thought that in order to achieve a measureable gain in strength, you only needed to focus on increasing the maximum amount of weight a given muscle group could lift for one repetition. The truth is that strength gains can be achieved by creating many types of changes. These changes challenge to a muscle group and promote adaptation. Even if you are increasing the weight you are lifting in a 3-rep, 8-rep or 15-rep bracket, you are getting stronger.

Gaining strength is all relative to where you began. If you start your weight lifting efforts lifting 100 pounds for 3 sets of 10 reps, and 2 weeks later you are now lifting 110 pounds for 3 sets of 10 reps, you accomplished a 10 percent increase in strength. This is one basic example and there is more than to learn about continuously improving your strength and ultimately martial art skills.

One-rep-max training (or absolute strength training) is one of the most commonly known strength training formats. However, it is out-dated as a stand-alone method of training. Although growth of the muscle may occur, a progressive strength training program involves structured change. This change must be thoughtful and also be applied to the format, routines, brackets, intensity and exercises of a program. Today, strength training encompasses more than one simple program type. You will read in the next chapters how the principles of training offer a macro-view of your strength training program. Learning how to apply these principles and design our own program will be of great value. Since the typical martial artist trains and possibly competes all year with no precise off-season (off-season as a period of time that is no less than 4 weeks and lasts up to 12 weeks), it is critical to follow a strength training program that balances the need for rest and recovery. Additionally, I distinguish between absolute strength (or, one-rep-max) workouts and those focused on enhancing functional strength for dynamic sports like martial arts. Improvements in your functional sport strength will prove to be a very rewarding process. Most of the programs in this book focus on workouts that translate immediately into improving martial arts skill sets. I will always acknowledge the need for strength to translate into dynamic power and speed for movements like stances, punches, blocks, throws and kicks. The pursuit of one does not exclude the other.

As a martial artist, you should view adding strength training to your routine as the pursuit of improving overall strength and performance for the functional application of your sport, while promoting the health of your joints. In this book, I present methods of strength training with the goal of helping you achieve sport-specific results, all the while keeping in mind the need for overall well-being and health.

HOW DOES STRENGTH TRAINING HELP YOU LOSE WEIGHT?

There are many ways to organize your strength training program in order to achieve noticeable gains in muscle size or a leaner physique. If one of your goals is to become leaner, decrease your body fat, increase your lean muscle mass and improve your metabolism, this book will serve you well.

Most people associate only doing cardiovascular exercises with the best method of weight loss. Truth be told, strength training will help you lose weight. As mentioned above, muscle tissue is highly active and requires a lot of calories in order to rebuild, repair and grow after a rigorous strength training workout. As more muscle tissue is built and the body's composition changes from more fat to more muscle, the metabolism increases and the body burns more calories overall. When you combine this benefit with the fact that hypertrophy (growth or leaning-out of the muscle) also occurs from a well-designed strength training program, you are more likely to achieve your aesthetic goals.

After a few months of regular strength training, you will experience improvements in the shape of your muscles. The integration of strength exercises into your existing martial arts program will serve as an investment in your metabolic score, so to speak. As more muscle is developed indicating improvement in lean body mass, your body will burn more calories. There is an estimated 15% increase in your metabolism when weight training is performed a few times a week.

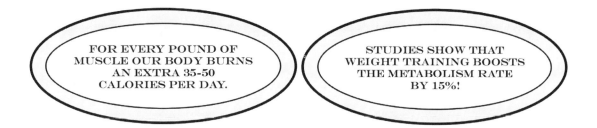

FOR EVERY POUND OF MUSCLE OUR BODY BURNS AN EXTRA 35-50 CALORIES PER DAY.

STUDIES SHOW THAT WEIGHT TRAINING BOOSTS THE METABOLISM RATE BY 15%!

IMPORTANCE OF STRENGTHENING CONNECTIVE TISSUE

You are not just made up of skeletal muscles. In fact, your muscle serves two primary functions: 1) to perform contractions causing the body to move, and 2) to create stability for the entire body. Both of these functions actually involve your connective tissue. Connective tissue is actually the supportive structure that muscle is built upon. When it is ignored, injuries are far more likely to occur. If absolute strength is the primary focus and exercises are chosen that only pursue heavy lifting, the functionality of the muscle will be compromised and ultimately weakened. Despite possible size enhancements that occur as a result of the exercises, strength training must serve to strengthen the body from the inside out. All programs must integrate exercises that improve balance, promote mobility and joint stability. This translates into strengthening connective tissue. This is discussed further in the section on joint stability. As you apply the information from each chapter and scan the various workouts provided in the programs section, it will become clear why many of the routines have infused movements that enhance the health of the connective tissue, as it relates to your muscle and joint structure.

DEVELOPING POWER AND STRENGTH

*"The magic of power training is that
improvements can occur quickly and it does
promote fat burning post-workout."*

Many fitness professionals get a chuckle from the trendy products and workout programs that gain temporary national fame. Often, trendy fitness fads are gadget-driven and shallow, therefore, lacking long-term weight loss benefits. But currently, it has become trendy to train for power. Power training is an absolutely valid and a worthwhile fad to follow, and most of the information circulating about fat burning benefits is correct.

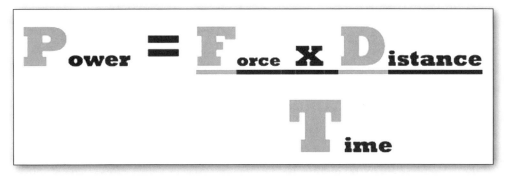

The mathematical explanation of power training is worth learning. It is simply force multiplied by velocity, or more specifically, force x distance/time. It is in looking at this equation that it is easiest to understand how it differs from strength training. Strength training manipulates just mass (movement of a load). Power training is dynamic in its very nature, and therefore it requires time and acceleration. Power exercises require velocity; therefore, improving power can also increase speed. Examples of this are a fighter whose hand speed increases or a forms competitor who is able to add an additional kick in rotation when jumping and spinning. One great exercise for this could be box jumps that progress into weighted jumps onto a box, with a controlled step down (see plyometrics section for guidelines).

Despite the variances between all the martial arts, I rarely meet a martial arts practitioner that does not value a punch packed with power. If this is the case, you want to train to improve power. Athletic power training can be packaged many ways. In short, explosive exercises that last 10 or 20 seconds, or sets that progress repetitions rapidly, develop power. They can be formatted in repetitive sets, or as part of a circuit. The common goal in any of these types of training modules is improving the amount of force exerted in each repetition. For example, to enhance punching power, one can perform 20 seconds of medicine ball slams against a wall (see ballistics section for guidelines), then immediately do a set of clap pushups, followed by punching.

There are several approaches to adding power training to your martial arts routine. Some believe that power training should separately train velocity and force before integrating them, and others combine them immediately. The magic of power training is that improvements can occur quickly and it does promote fat-burning post-workout. I am aware that this last statement makes it sound like power training is the solution we have all been looking for to accomplish weight loss and improve Lean Body Mass (LBM). Unfortunately, you cannot perform power workouts all year round and alongside all martial arts training sessions. You must change your routine periodically (see periodization section for guidelines) in order to avoid injuries and maximize the benefits of every workout program.

The success of power training and weight loss is present when it is properly implemented into your entire training routine, which includes time to recover and regular changes. Additionally, power training follows logical rules of progression to promote overall improvements. Understanding progression and trying to gauge your personal intensity level will directly impact the success of your martial arts training comprehensively. Strength training programs, whether they feature power drills, plyometrics, or one-rep-max formats, only have merit if they keep you injury free.

I am going to propose a couple categories of power training. Not everyone needs to separate them, but it may help you to better apply concepts of power training to your training program. Breaking power training down can assist you in choosing which exercises will improve specific elements of your martial arts skills. Classifying them can also help you choose the most appropriate power exercises so you do not cause injuries. There are many power exercises that will increase martial arts explosivity. Whether your goal is to improve your demonstration of powerful kicks for a belt test, reaction time for sprawling or your punching power, ballistics, plyometrics and strength exercises will enhance your overall athletic skill sets in martial arts. Although they can be organized into different workout programs, they do not need to be trained exclusive of each other.

BALLISTIC EXERCISES

Ballistics exercises have tremendous velocity and involve the muscles producing the greatest amount of force in the shortest amount of time. In fact, you want acceleration throughout this type of training exercise. The speed and force of the movement outweighs the actual weight or mass. A classic example of a ballistic exercise is medicine ball training. It is valuable for all martial artists. For example, it improves punching power. It can help with learning how to breathe and integrates the core. The medicine ball can be used for drills like overhead throws, or in a sport specific manner like throwing it in a straight line against a wall to improve punches. By performing this type of medicine ball pass against a concrete wall, you will develop power while reinforcing the muscular involvement needed when throwing punches. The medicine ball itself may only need to weight 6, 8 or 10 pounds, but you are expected to throw the ball with far more than 10 pounds of force, and your speed should increase throughout your interval (or set).

PLYOMETRIC EXERCISES

Plyometric exercises are very popular as a form of power training. These types of exercises involve pushing the muscles to quickly load and unload with acceleration for short intervals of time. The goal of plyometric exercises is to create the strongest contraction in the shortest amount of time. They involve high speeds during a movement and are complex in that they usually involve many joints of the body.

Plyometrics exercises improve power because they summon the stretch reflex before the muscle contracts. This stretching of the muscle occurs before the muscular contraction, which allows it to contract with greater force. Exercises that involve speed and consistent movement are ideal. This can include box jumps, jumping knee tucks, broad jumps, jump squats or single leg hops. If you notice, these examples are all jumps. Therefore, you will find that plyometric exercises are often referred to as jump training.

The American Council on Exercise (ACE) offers very clear recommendations for plyometric training. Because of the impact, jump drills require balance and control when landing. Therefore, plyometrics are not ideal for those who have orthopedic limitations. The landing forces can cause injury to those who are in poor shape or have suffered an injury. Since so many of us have incurred an injury from training at some point, it is important to understand how to progress, how to choose appropriate exercises, and how to gauge your intensity level. If you are eager to include plyometrics in your martial athletic routine, but you recently have suffered an injury, check with your physical therapist or doctor. One place to start is with strength training and joint stability exercises. By improving functional sport and absolute strength in a total body routine as is suggested by the National Strength and Conditioning Association (NCSA), you will more easily prepare the body for jump training. Other suggestions made by the NSCA are listed below:

NSCA's Guidelines for Plyometric Training

- Depth jumps (jumping off a platform higher than 18 inches) are not ideal for most people. It is recommended to avoid if you weight over 220 pounds.

- Do not perform complex high intensity plyometrics workouts on consecutive days. Allow 2-4 days of rest.

- Do not perform your plyometric sets when you are fatigued.

- Insert appropriate rest in-between intervals to avoid injury.

- Learn to land. A soft landing is an important technical component to successful plyometric training.

- Footwear is important and a slip-free landing surface will help to prevent injuries.

- Properly warm up, do not begin with plyometrics, in fact preparing the body with lower intensity exercises similar in movement to your jump drills may lead to better performance (i.e. squats, lunges, rope jump, dynamic stretching).

- If you feel pain in your back or joint stop immediately.

summarized from NSCA

Strength training can incorporate exercises that have explosive characteristics. For example, kettlebell training has a dynamic integration of the core and balance, while requiring large muscles to be recruited and multiple joints to be involved. There are many strength training programs and weight exercises that promote hypertrophy (or muscle growth), offer a measurable increase in strength and develop power. Some of my favorite power and strength workouts are in the programs section at the end of the book. I have improved my martial arts skills by using many of these exercises over my 30+ years of training.

STRENGTHENING YOUR JOINTS

*"..recreating instability, teaches
the body how to become stable."*

The martial arts are unique because balance training is constantly being applied during all stages of practice. Like a dancer or gymnast on a balance beam, martial artists spend a lot of their time on one leg or even avoiding being thrown. This explicit act should motivate all martial artists to place more emphasis on joint stability for themselves and their students. In doing so, you will be improving the overall health of the connective tissue throughout the body.

Joint stability and mobility is more than just practicing to balance on one leg. It is the way in which you integrate strength exercises that challenge your overall balance and aid the joint in withstanding shock and preventing injury. The connective tissue of the body serves as the support structure for the muscle, like the frame of a house being held together by bricks and mortar. Joint stability training will strengthen connective tissue. The addition of exercises that place the body in an unstable position while adding a progression of dynamic movement forces the joints to react, adjust and balance. Simply put, recreating instability, teaches the body how to become stable. A simple example with a progression is to perform dumbbell bicep curls on one leg. Then progress to standing with 2 feet on a wobble board while curling, then one foot on a wobble board. This exercise series will not only be an exercise for the biceps, but will help to strengthen the joints and connective tissue in the leg.

Although joint mobility and stability are being presented as a unit above, they do have separate definitions. If joint stability is tangibly thought of as balance, then mobility is the amount the joint can move. The joint's mobility is tied as closely to the word "flexibility" as it is to "stability". Joint stability and mobility coexist, and therefore, when speaking of one, I am automatically including the value of the other. Joint stability and mobility together lead to efficient, healthy and safe movement. Therefore, when you perform exercises that improve joint stability or flexibility, the mobility of the joints involved is also improving from the exercise..

TYPES OF JOINTS IN THE BODY:

- BALL AND SOCKET (i.e. the shoulder)
- PIVOT (i.e. the neck)
- HINGE (i.e. elbow)

Like all aspects of training, an appropriate starting point should be identified and a progression should be created as you improve your balancing skills and increase strength. The joints of the body (all 360 of them) rely on neuromuscular communication, which is actually an unconscious response. This is also called proprioception. Proprioceptive information is a feedback system that is run by the brain, telling it to stabilize the joints when the body is in action. It is used for every movement a martial artist performs. Stability training can offer preventative injury benefits as well. Even a handful of joint stability exercises every week can help avoid or lessen the severity of an injury.

Sections of the body and the Placement of 360 Joints of the body:

<u>Vertebral Column Spinal Area and Back)-147 joints total</u>

25 joints between the vertebra

72 joints between the vertebra and ribs

<u>Thorax (Chest Area) – 24 joints total</u>

2 joints between the sternum and thoracic cage (chest)

18 joints between the sternum and ribs

2 joints between the clavicle and the scapulae (shoulder blades)

2 joints between the scapulae (shoulder blades) and thorax

<u>Upper Body – 86 joints total</u>

2 joints between the scapular bones (shoulder blades)

6 joints between the elbows

8 joints between the wrists

70 joints between the hand bones

<u>Lower Body – 92 joints total</u>

2 joints in the hips

6 joints between the knee bones

6 joints between the ankles

74 joints throughout the feet bones

<u>Pelvis- 11 joints total</u>

4 joints between the coccyx vertebrae (tailbone)

6 joints between the acetabulum (hip)

1 joint at the pubic symphysis (pubic bone)

How does the joint know when to balance?

Joints are located where two bones come together and are supported by ligaments and tendons. These surround the muscles and protect the joint from injury. They fire a signal to the brain, which in turn is received and relayed to the ligaments and tendons so that they can react when any stress is felt. A vulnerable joint is considered one with poor stability, weak connective tissue or little proprioceptive abilities. Thankfully, all of these characteristics are trainable and joints can become stronger if there has been damage to even the ligaments and tendons.

What are the common joint injuries in the martial arts?

Sprained ankles, shoulders, back and twisted knees are the most common mild injuries that easily develop into long-term chronic and nagging pain. For this reason, it is important to add some of the basic stability exercises (listed in the Exercises section) into your routine for preventative measure. These types of weakness are common within the martial arts community. It is common for all types of martial arts practitioners to experience a stumble when sparring or an accidental ankle roll from a jump kick. But with 360 joints in the body, it feels like an overwhelming task to tend to them all, while still engaging in a total body strength training program and martial arts practice. Most strength and conditioning coaches and physical therapists expect their athletes to focus mostly on the larger joints when incorporating joint stability exercises. They often design strength training routines that automatically integrate various methods of enhancing proprioception. The best way to incorporate joint stability exercises into your routine is to choose a couple of exercises and insert them into a warm up or use equipment that offers a balance challenge (i.e. kettlebells, BOSU, cable machines, resist-a-ball).

BODYWEIGHT TRAINING FOR THE MARTIAL ATHLETE
by Ryan Hoover, Owner of Co-Founder of Fit-to-Fight

No field is rifer with fads, crazes and trends, than the fitness industry. The latest mania barely hits the infomercial circuit before the new "next big thing" is the buzz on talk shows, in fitness mags and in the big box fitness centers. However, the one constant throughout the storied (and often infamous) evolution of fitness has been bodyweight training—the use of one's body in natural movements to provide resistance. This is especially true for combat sports. Over time, other modalities (which certainly have merit) sometimes garner more praise, since the less experienced trainers may underestimate the "simplicity" of bodyweight movements, but "natural" training has always had a place.

To be a successful combat athlete, you must employ more than just the practice of your art or sport. Balance and the ability to move quickly while performing complex techniques, often under physical and emotional stress, is one of the most functional athletic needs for a successful martial arts career. A common lesson taught in the martial arts is that you must have command of every aspect of your body if you are to ever have control over another's body. Bodyweight training is one method of training that will help you to achieve this control.

There are numerous body weight exercises. Beyond their functional application, they are safe, convenient, and natural. They offer training totality.

Safety – Bodyweight training is normally more forgiving on the joints, once the basic movements are properly learned. Since the martial arts can already be taxing on the joints, incorporating body weight strength training can help prevent injuries. Also, because the movements tend to be more natural, this modality prepares the martial athlete mentally. You will feel more confident about your abilities to perform most martial movements with minimized risk (i.e. throws, ground fighting, and clinch work).

Convenience – There is no gear required for this modality. However, gear may be added to enhance or progress some movements for more advanced athletes. This makes the training inexpensive (i.e. free) and very portable. It also makes it readily available for personal training or group training, alike.

Natural – Bodyweight movements are generally functional, meaning the exercises require the body to move as it would normally. This is especially important for the combat athlete, since self defense and/or fighting requires one to move in any and all directions, as opposed to the very linear (and typically unnatural) movements demanded by machines or free weights.

"Complete" – With most bodyweight movements, muscle groups are "encouraged" to work together (which is innate) as opposed to in isolation. This does not mean training that isolates muscle groups is undesirable, but if training time is very limited, and for most people it is, this sort of training tends to be more practical. This is why most martial art schools have always relied on push-ups, pull-ups and dips to accomplish upper body strengthening in their classes. These movements also allow stabilizing muscles to be strengthened. This makes for a true total body workout and builds a powerful core (the center of force and strength for the combat athlete).

Progressive – While most modalities are progressive, typical strength training involves, and is primarily limited to, simply adding more weight. With bodyweight training, multiple progression options are not only available, but are relatively easy to implement.

Here are a few tips that may help increase your understanding of how to incorporate body weight exercises into your workout program:

- Advanced Variations and/or Increased Resistance=Increases in Strength and Size.
- Start slowly and listen to your body.
- Begin by adding two days of bodyweight training per week. (this will vary by the individual and one should consider other types of training that are being utilized.)
- Fast twitch fibers tend to have the greatest potential for growth, so if size is part of the goal, repetitions should be between 4 and 10 for most exercises.
- Basic progressions should involve increased sets, repetitions or time, along with exercise variations.

ABOUT RYAN HOOVER

Ryan Hoover is Fit to Fight® co-founder (www.ftfcenters.com) and the Chief FTF® Krav Maga instructor. He is a 2nd degree black belt in Krav Maga and has black belts in multiple systems. He has co-authored three books on Krav Maga including:

- Krav Maga for Beginners
- Black Belt Krav Maga
- Krav Maga for Women

Ryan is also a certified natural trainer and a speed, agility and quickness trainer. He has worked with a wide range of athletes and actors. Some of his clients include:

- Revolution actor, Tracy Spiridakos
- Revolution actor, Daniella Alonso
- Stuntwoman of the Year, Alicia Vela-Bailey
- Carolina Panthers Head Coach, Ron Rivera
- Chicago Bears Linebacker, James Anderson
- Carolina Panthers defensive end, Charles Johnson
- Carolina Panthers tight end, Greg Olsen
- Carolina Panthers special teams captain, Jordan Senn
- Carolina Panthers strength and conditioning coach, Joe Kenn

Ryan is also the co-founder of the self-protection program, Hard Ready, Pride-the Kids Program, and Safer Campus Now-active shooter defense program. Ryan is a Krav Maga Force Training instructor, as well as a Krav Maga Train the Trainer. He has trained instructors in over 8 different countries. He has been instrumental in developing defensive tactics curricula at the state level. Ryan owns two training centers in North Carolina called Fit-to-Fight

DOES STRENGTH TRAINING MAKE YOU BETTER AT MARTIAL ARTS?
by RJ Cohen, Co-Owner of Cohen Judo Club

Strength training in regards to martial arts is a very complicated subject and the answer is different for each category of practitioner. Also, strength training in itself is a very complicated subject as everybody has his or her own opinion of what actual strength training truly involves. My expertise in the martial arts is primarily in grappling martial arts such as judo, wrestling and jiu-jitsu. I have spent time with martial artists of all kind, but my legacy has been Olympic judo and the arts that support that style of practice. It is my philosophy that strength training is not just about getting strong; strength training involves the combination of strength, speed, power, balance, coordination and flexibility.

Strength training is extremely important in martial arts, and creating the right strength training program will absolutely make you a better martial artist and help you create a healthier lifestyle in the years after hard-core training, competition or full-time instruction. I was introduced to strength training early in my martial arts career. I spent time learning proper form and credit this time understanding how to integrate strength training into my full-time judo program as the reason I have virtually had an injury-free career. Proper strength training will greatly reduce the risk of injury. However, I have also seen many martial artists create strength training routines that are way too specific to their martial art, and therefore, lack the general strength necessary to be an explosive athlete.

I believe that the time doing martial arts should be separate from your strength training. When you strength train, your ultimate goal should focus on getting your body stronger, faster, and more flexible and when you are training in martial arts, your ultimate goal should focus on improving your martial art or sport. The separation of these two components does not mean they will not overlap.

Everybody is genetically different and some people are going to be naturally stronger. Others will be naturally more explosive. These natural abilities should be kept in mind when designing your strength training program. One time I worked with a top judo player and he was 30 pounds lighter than me, and yet, he was the strongest person I have ever felt. I asked him what he does in his workouts. I was shocked that it did not incorporate any strength training at all. Although I believe he would still benefit from strength training as a regular part of his overall training routine, it made me realize that genetics are powerful too.

Choosing my favorite strength training exercises for judo players is complicated. Here is a list of my favorite strength exercises:

power lifting	all core stabilization
plyometric training	Olympic lifting
heavy rope climbing	pull-ups & push-ups
speed drills	flexibility training

My absolute favorite exercise for judo is rope climbing. I have consistently seen it done at International judo training centers and universities all over the world. It is the one exercise across the board that has improved the strength of my judo students.

ABOUT RJ COHEN

RJ Cohen comes from a long-line of accomplished judo players. Currently the co-Owner of the Cohen Brothers Training Center in Illinois (http://cohensjudoclub.com). His school was founded by his father, Irwin and uncle Steve in 1992. RJ was born into a strong judo legacy. Both his father and uncle were Olympic competitors and coaches for the US Olympic team (his father won the Bronze Medal in Munich Games in 1972). RJ competed from 1998 until 2008, winning a wide variety of titles including US Senior Nationals, Jr, Pan AM Championships and US Sr Open. Today, RJ coaches judo at the National level and runs a wrestling program along with his brother for Illinois state competitors. He is an advocate of cross-training and integrates high intensity interval training and strength training into his elite judo program.

FLEXIBILITY TRAINING ENHANCES STRENGTH

Many people view flexibility as simply sitting and stretching. Martial artists are made aware of the value of flexibility early on in their training. In fact, martial arts are one of the rare sports that place an appropriate emphasis on flexibility exercises compared to many other mainstream sports. Punches, stances and kicks do promote healthy joint mobility and range of motion. However, even long-time students of the martial arts will experience tightening and shortening of the muscles at some point in time. If unaddressed, injuries may arise. All martial artists should regularly reevaluate their flexibility training methods. It is important to add purposeful flexibility exercises to prevent muscle stiffness, soreness and injuries. This effort will also help achieve an elongated muscular state and maximize strength training efforts.

Flexibility training is the use of movement to promote the joint's full range of motion while also lengthening the muscles involved. There are two primary methods of flexibility training that I will promote throughout this book that best apply to martial arts training: dynamic flexibility and static flexibility. There are other variations of flexibility, but they are mostly utilized in a clinical setting or with a trainer.

Dynamic flexibility, commonly called functional flexibility is intended to improve range of motion and lengthen muscles with controlled movement at varying speeds. Static flexibility improves range of motion and lengthens muscles without any velocity, and is usually a held position. Despite the value placed on having good flexibility for kicks and stances, the martial artist needs to understand the differences between the various methods of improving flexibility in order to avoid injuries. Aside from the clinical methods of improving flexibility, dynamic and static training efforts must keep you within a safe or pain-free zone.

Static Flexibility

In many traditional martial arts schools, flexibility training has been characterized by simply dropping down into the splits. This is an example of static flexibility. Static flexibility is sometimes also called slow or isometric. For our purposes, I will only refer to it as static. Static flexibility exercises can also be viewed as positions. They are generally a specific posture or stance that is held for a specific period of time. The splits, butterfly stretch or horse stance are technically static positions that will affect the involvement of the joint's range of motion and muscle length. Often in these positions, gravity is the outside force that is being used to accomplish a deeper position. Traditional yoga, like hatha and many martial arts have relied mostly on static flexibility. It has been found to be successful in improving range of motion, but static stretching should always be applied with a controlled effort and no velocity. Controversies surrounding the effectiveness of static stretching mostly center around three basic arguments:

1.) Prolonged static stretching has been related to minor connective tissue damage (Laban, 1962; Sapega et al., 1981; Warren, et al., 1971 and 1976, Science of Flexibility, p.159).
2.) Static stretches do not increase body temperature, which is critical when preparing the body for any workout.
3.) Static stretches do not recreate the nature of athletic movement.

Although I do suggest using static stretches in your martial arts training and strength training routines, I find they have less value before a warm-up. Additionally, many rituals in the martial arts incorporate static stretches, and therefore, remain relevant. It is common that students gather before a class begins and sit in various poses (i.e. seated V or butterfly). But to maximize your stretching efforts, static stretches serve more as a means to reinforce the proper technique for many poses and positions in the martial arts. They are not the optimal method for increasing a joint's range of motion for the dynamic practice of punches, kicks, sprawls, throws and forms.

Dynamic Flexibility

Dynamic flexibility is required in all sports and activities included in your daily life. Therefore, it is often called functional flexibility. An exciting demonstration of dynamic flexibility that integrates a classic mainstream athletic skill set is when you watch a wide receiver zig zag down the field and take a sharp leaping step to catch the ball. This action demonstrates dynamic sport specific flexibility, as well as agility and speed. An example of a non-sport movement that requires functional flexibility is when you drop something while carrying a bag of groceries and you quickly bend over and pick it up.

A martial artist's training must promote dynamic movement, as it leads to vitality. It is one key to being a healthy athlete. The expression "life is non-stop and we live in perpetual motion", supports my encouragement of dynamic flexibility in all strength and martial arts training programs. Dynamic flexibility is a reliable training technique that will enhance your martial arts skills and assist with improving strength. The criticisms mentioned surrounding static flexibility are actually the benefits of dynamic flexibility. Dynamic flexibility will increase the body's core temperature while providing healthy circulation to the muscles involved in the movement. It also mimics the very essence of being athletic and can be adapted to most sport-specific movements. An additional characteristic of dynamic flexibility that differentiates it from static training methods (and even several clinical methods) is that it has no held position at the end of the stretch movement. Instead of gravity being the force applied to the joint, there is velocity. The controlled movement is often repeated which is how the body's temperature and circulation are increased.

On a more detailed level, flexibility is multi-dimensional. It is more than just how far you can stretch. For example, if you are practicing a form, you will move quickly through various stances, hold specific poses (or stances) and execute punches and kicks at a variety of speeds. This requires a tremendous amount of strength and power, as well as flexibility. Siff, M.C., and Verkhoshansky, Y.V. (1999) best explain the relationship between these elements. In fact, they created four clear definitions to better understand functional stretching and conditioning (see graphic below).

Types of Flexibility

• Static Flexibility - the range of motion of the joint without continuous movement. <u>Examples:</u> The splits or holding a horse stance.

• Dynamic Flexibility – the range of motion with controlled movement. Speed of movement is usually slow to medium. Interchanged today with the term functional flexibility. <u>Examples:</u> A fan kick or crescent kick.

• Ballistic Flexibility - range of motion of the joint with a bouncing or bobbing movement, usually differentiated from dynamic by its lack of control. The movement is not controlled at the stopping point of the action and occurs at medium to fast speeds. <u>Examples:</u> Arm rotations backwards without control.

• Passive Flexibility- the range of motion when another person passively moves your limb or articulates a part of your body. This type of flexibility does not include an active contraction. <u>Examples:</u> When a physical therapist moves your arm throughout your shoulder joint or a trainer stretches your hamstring.

The four categories are an in-depth look at how various applications of flexibility are needed in the martial arts. The strength of the muscles and joint stability play a critical role in healthy dynamic flexibility.

1) Flexibility, where speed is the ability to have full range of motion at medium to fast speeds.

2) Flexibility, where strength is the ability to have efficient and powerful movement throughout a full range of motion when doing a static or dynamic action or exercise.

3) Flexibility, where endurance is the ability to produce efficient range of motion when doing static and dynamic actions over and over again. This implies the movement is repetitive.

<u>Dynamic Flexibility is not the Same as Ballistic Flexibility</u>

Dynamic flexibility has been referred to as ballistic, fast or kinetic. Most of the literature draws little distinction between dynamic and ballistic. I believe they are completely different methods of flexibility training. As you will later read in the program design section, dynamic flexibility, and not ballistic should be part of every martial arts and strength training workout. Ballistic movements include velocity as they move through a range of motion, and there is no hold at the ending position; but they have little control. I characterize these movements as careless or reckless. Dynamic flexibility movements on the other hand, employ a controlled effort. To better clarify the distinction, imagine two wooden carts A and B, built exactly the same. Both are launched across the ground with the same force and actually travel the same distance. A is launched on a track and B with nothing controlling its direction. The demonstration with A is a dynamic movement. B travels in a ballistic manner and perhaps it wiggles and appears unstable as it travels. Because it was launched with nothing to help control it, more torque is placed on the nuts and bolts that hold it together. Your body experiences a similar response.

A ballistic action is when you carelessly move your arms and legs. There is less muscular control, and therefore, you are more likely to cause damage to connective tissue, muscle, ligaments and tendons. The potential for damage to the tissue and muscles that surround a joint is the primary criticism of ballistic flexibility. Once ballistic actions are separated from dynamic ones, there are less incidences of injury. The martial arts at its very core are not only intended to be dynamic, but also fluid. Flexibility training efforts should reinforce this mind-body connection. In doing so, dynamic flexibility will lead to successful martial arts and strength training.

Assessing Flexibility

It is important that our joints have a healthy and appropriate range of motion. Ranges of motion standards do exist. They are used in the clinical context, and often goniometry is used to measure the linear units or the degree of arc of a joint. But it is not necessary to use this tool when assessing your own flexibility and where improvements may be necessary. Furthermore, flexibility is not a general characteristic in the body like cardiovascular fitness. Range of motion will differ from joint to joint, and right to left side within a person's body. Regardless of the cause, there is no such score or way to quantify someone's total body flexibility. Truth be told, the methods used to measure flexibility from one physical therapist to another varies. Clinicians mostly rely on a skillful subjective review and overall clinical assessment of how range of motion in specific areas is impacting the overall function of the body. Some of their methods can be learned and answering these questions will help you assess your own flexibility:

1. Is any compensation being made by other areas of the body in order for the joint to move fully?
2. Does the joint have full range without pain? If there is pain, is it at the beginning phase of the range, or at the very end?
3. Is there a large discrepancy between the right and left side on the same joint (i.e. the right shoulder verse the left shoulder)?

For martial artists, flexibility needs should be determined on an individual basis, because some styles of martial arts require more flexibility than others. For example, tae kwon do and tai chi utilize flexibility very differently. Although both styles need what I would call "above average" flexibility, devoted practitioners in these styles have characteristic movements that simply require different types of flexibility. And, according to Siff, M.C., and Verkhoshansky, Y.V. (1999) definitions, a martial artist who practices mostly explosive kicks relies on flexibility that covers all 3 categories: strength, speed and endurance, verse a tai chi student that moves fluidly and slowly into poses, requiring flexible endurance and strength.

Are Stretching Devices Valuable?

There are few technological breakthroughs in flexibility training that warrant the need for flexibility equipment. Although the various machines or gadgets on the market may assist you in gaining a deeper position when holding a stretch, the method of increasing your "stretch angle" often causes more muscle damage and may even limit mobility. Flexibility training is best done by your own independent efforts so that you can be responsive to pain. Furthermore, when using a stretching device, positional adjustments are made to simply increase the angle of the joint. Using gadgets usually leads to a superficial increase in your range of motion and has little benefit when you are moving dynamically during your martial arts practice. Flexibility equipment may force you to compromise your position, posture or pelvic placement.

There are a handful of useful tools that you can utilize to assist you with static flexibility. The tools I recommend are yoga blocks, straps, tubing, foam rollers and resist-a-balls. These can help you improve flexibility and prevent injuries while maintaining control of your body's position. When using these types of tools, remember that they are there to provide you with additional support. To maximize the benefits of all flexibility exercises, you need to maintain proper body alignment and continue to breathe.

PART II

GETTING STARTED

*"Everyone sits somewhere on an athletic continuum
that encompasses all athletic strengths,
weaknesses and skills."*

USE YOUR DISCIPLINE NATURE TO FIND TIME TO STRENGTH TRAIN

In order to best apply training concepts from this book, you need to set yourself up to succeed. I find that allotting time to workout is the biggest struggle people face. Even if you are making it to your martial arts school a couple times a week, finding an additional 20-45 minutes for strength training will require time management skills. These skills fall under the category of discipline. The very foundation of practicing martial arts is discipline. Harness the discipline you have for practicing martial arts, and apply it to your strength training needs.

5 QUESTIONS TO ASK BEFORE GETTING STARTED

Although the other parts of this book are far more comprehensive than this chapter, it might be the most practical content. I believe that everyone sits somewhere on an athletic continuum that encompasses all athletic strengths, weaknesses and skills. If you are aware of your strengths and weaknesses, you must then understand how to focus your training efforts. If this is you and you only know ten exercises, you will have a more productive strength training experience than an individual with access to a fully equipped weight room that is unaware of his or her position on an athletic continuum. Even professional trainers use a continuum of sorts to assess how to approach their client's needs and goals. As your own personal trainer, you need to become familiar with the athletic continuum.

Part V of this book provides a number of strength and conditioning programs. Not all of them will be viable programs or exercises for you at the beginning. The exercises you select and the intensity you perform them should be congruent with your goals as a martial artist. I realize that almost everyone reading this book wants to increase strength and improve his or her lean body mass, martial arts skills and possibly performance. Although some of these goals will stay the same, many will evolve as you begin using this book.

Since you are going to serve as your own personal trainer, you need to follow the same protocol of a responsible fitness trainer. You are going to interview yourself. To begin the process of designing a strength and conditioning program, it is best to answer a handful of questions. The answers to these telling questions will provide structure and clarity that will help you realize which exercises are the most appropriate. It will also reveal the intensity, repetition bracket (i.e. 12-15 reps, 10-12 reps, or 8-6 reps) and style of sets (i.e. timed intervals or a number of sets) that are most appropriate. Do not try to implement too many changes or combine too many programs at once. And most importantly, be honest with yourself about the level of experience you have with strength training.

Question 1:
Where will I workout?

Once you have decided if you are training at the gym, your home or your martial arts school, you will be able to refine the list of exercises to reflect the equipment you have available. If you design your own strength training program or choose one from this book that exceeds the amount of time you have available, do not fret. Remember that every time you begin a new training program, it is like conducting a small experiment with your body. Every athlete will experience a strength program differently. For example, if a specific amount of time is allocated for rest and you require more rest before moving on to the next set of exercises, the program will simply take longer than the prescribed time.

Question 2:
How many minutes can I devote to strength training?

Ten-minute workout DVDs have become unbelievably popular. Although, these 10-minute workouts will have a positive impact on the body, you will be far more successful with a minimum of 20 minutes of strength training. Ten minutes of strength training will not provide the body with a sufficient warm up. Twenty-minute workouts at least offer 3 to 5 minutes of mobility exercises that can prevent injuries from the 15 minutes of high intensity or challenging strength training that follows.

On the other hand, more than 60 minutes of strength training is unnecessary. Compile a list of exercises that fit into the amount of time you realistically can carve out of your schedule.

Question 3:
What injuries or weaknesses would I like to address?

Everyone is aware of weaknesses. It could be that your sidekick has always been challenging because you have weak gluteal muscles and poor inner thigh flexibility. Or, maybe you have always been very quick, but lack general strength. Or, perhaps your back requires extra warming up because you sit during your job all day. Knowing this about yourself is the key to your long-term training success. It will also help you become aware of your position on an athletic continuum. By addressing these weaknesses immediately and regularly, you will be able to benefit comprehensively from any form of strength training including weight training, kettlebell or bodyweight exercises. When you honestly address your weaknesses, you are more likely to prevent them from developing into injuries. This will help you to maximize other efforts you make in improving your overall strength and conditioning.

Question 4:
What are my strengths as an athletic individual?

There is an athletic continuum for the development of strength, speed, power and flexibility. We all sit closer to one side than the other side on this continuum. For example, you might be a very strong judo player, but you lose your steam quickly in a match. Or, you may have great height in your kicks when doing your forms, but they lack strength. Knowing your strengths will also help you properly focus your training. Do not mistake this for being given a pass on training all athletic elements including your strengths. If you are a naturally explosive martial artist, then the number of weeks or number of exercises you spend in a power phase might be less than the weeks and exercises dedicated to building general strength. A well-designed program will always pay tribute to your strengths as an athlete and constantly address potential weaknesses.

Question 5:
What level of experience do I have with strength training?

If you are a novice and just starting your strength training endeavors, focus on general strength and hold off on more advanced exercises or programs. Remember there is nothing wrong with the basics. There is a top ten list of exercises I suggest to every newcomer to strength training. These are the first exercises to learn if you lack experience. I believe they will provide you with a valuable strength-training foundation. Mastering the technique of these exercises will set you up to be able to workout in any environment. The biomechanics of these exercises (or proper technical alignment) will also make learning advanced exercises easier and provide you with many variations when increasing the intensity. This list of top ten exercises can progress by adding dumbbells, kettlebells, cables, straight bars, plate loaded racking systems, nautilus equipment, suspension straps and resistance tubing.

Top 10 Exercises for Newcomers to Strength Training

1. Lunge/Box Squats
2. Chest Press
3. Lat Pull Down
4. Row - Standing or Seated
5. Pushup/Plank
6. Chest Fly
7. Pelvic Bridges
8. Cable Chop (any variation)
9. Ball Crunches
10. Arm Raises/Fly (all directions: front, side, off-angle, overhead, rear)

If you are an advanced exerciser and looking for new ways to diversify your martial arts training, then you will need a highlighter as you read through the exercises and programs sections of this book. You will find the majority of the exercises and programs to be suitable. However, the four other questions are still a useful exercise when designing a new strength training program. They will provide you with objectivity and help you organize how the exercises you choose fit into various strength training phases.

THE MOST IMPORTANT PART OF WARMING UP

The martial arts, like dance, require the practice of its movements on the right and left sides of the body. Because of this, and the nature of movements like kicks and stances, the martial arts have dynamic flexibility embedded within its training. For example, when you are practicing kicks at both a controlled and quick pace, you are improving the range of motion of the hip joint and lengthening the muscles connected and involved in the action. Despite the nature of practicing martial arts movements, and the fact that the joints of the legs and arms travel through larger ranges of motion than bowling, hockey or tennis, does not mean that an organized flexibility program is less relevant when training the martial arts.

One of the best places to integrate structured flexibility and functional movement training is in the beginning of a workout. Dynamic flexibility and functional movements should account for a large portion of your warm up. This combination will translate into the very nature of all martial arts movements and develop stability, mobility and flexibility.

Static flexibility although useful, should not be the only form of flexibility used in the beginning section of your training program. I believe that static stretching exercises are overused in the martial arts. Static stretches are more appropriately placed at the end of a workout or as part of a cool down. They can also be used as a holding pattern (an active rest or transition) for the body, or as a tool for meditation and breathing post-workout.

WHAT IS THE BEST WAY TO WARM UP?

A proper warm up can make or break your workout. I believe there are 5 primary objectives for a well-designed warm up. Since I never do a workout that has a narrow focus, like only strengthening my biceps or only sitting in a horse stance. My warm-ups include all five of these objectives:

1. Increase body temperature.
2. Increase blood flow to the large muscle groups.
3. Produce faster and more efficient muscle contractions in all areas being utilized.
4. Decrease injuries by increasing the elasticity of the muscles and the mobility of the joints using stability and flexibility exercises.
5. Mentally prepare the body for the workout ahead.

All five of these objectives are inter-related. The first one, leads to the second, which leads to the third and so on. Since most martial arts utilize all muscle groups and require most joints of the body to be involved, it is critical that your warm up is not limited to one single repetitive movement or a non-weight barring action. For example, a 5-minute power walk or a recumbent bike session does not require the arms and legs to move in a coordinated fashion or demand much balance. Although it might accomplish objective 1 and 2, and partially 3, I consider this type of warm up to be insubstantial. Walking or biking can be part of a warm up to accomplish 1 and 2, but I would follow up with some combination of weight barring exercises like squats, leg lifts and arm circles. Below is a guideline suggesting exercises that provide the body with an ideal warm up.

Over the years, most resources have advised that a warm up should reflect movements that will be included in your core workout. Although this is true, there are movements that are critical for all sports and offer the foundation for functional movement. Gray Cook, a Physical Therapist and Sports Conditioning Expert best articulated movements for functional mobility in several of his books. He identified 7 key movements. Although he uses them as a baseline for clinical evaluation, I believe most of them should be incorporated into every warm up or beginning section of a martial art, strength or athletic workout. The list of warm up exercises I have created below is influenced by Cook's recommendations.

Exercises from the movement categories below can be easily incorporated in every warm up:

- **Legs** – Bending, Changing Your Center of Gravity and Levels (i.e. Lunges and Squats)

  These exercises involve bending and extending of joints throughout the legs. Even if you are not moving quickly, it does require control over your center of gravity. Bending your knees causes your body to change level. It moves closer and further from the ground. Begin with 3-5 reps of each exercise. You can use them in a rhythmic fashion or as a simple movement set. They do not have to be executed at full range of motion, In fact, it is better to ease into the depth of these leg exercises.

- **Arms** – Reaching and Rotation (i.e. Arm Circles)

  These movements loosen up the shoulder joint and upper back for any form of intense upper body action. They can be combined with leg movements in a fluid sequence or be a basic combination of light shadow boxing that alternates with arm circles. Remember that the shoulder joint is a ball and socket joint and it should move in all directions.

- **Torso** – Rotation, Flexion and Extension (i.e. twisting or plank holds)

  These movements prepare the lower back and core for stabilizing during the workout. It will also assist in releasing tension or tightness that may be felt from sitting for long periods throughout the day. There are many martial arts movements like punching and blocking that combines thorough torso movement. If you use shadow boxing in a warm up at low intensity, it can provide an appropriate warm up interval. Or, you can move through various types of plank exercises that incorporate the legs moving towards the upper body (i.e. mountain climbers, alligators). Control your speed and form.

- **Balance** – Calve Contractions and Overall Joint Stability (i.e. calve raises or single leg balance)

  These types of movement prepare the ankles, feet and lower legs for actions like jumping and even kicking. I rely on all sorts of leg lifts for my warm up. It prepares my body on several levels: 1) I am transferring my weight and preparing for single leg balance movements 2) It offers dynamic flexibility and helps to heat up my muscle appropriately. 3) There are many variations of leg lifts that recruit all the muscles in the legs and surrounding joints.

The movements listed can be combined with various types of calisthenics, jump rope, cardio machines or sports drills. They can be dispersed through a workout routine as your training progresses; or be built into a fluid sequence with natural transitions. However you choose to implement these recommendations, your warm up for your strength training and martial arts workout must include complex movements, multiple joints, the upper and the lower body.

SAMPLE WARM UP 1:

- 10 jumping jacks
- 5 squats
- 10 alternating knee lifts
- 10 jumping jacks
- 5 squats with rotation on each side
- 10 alternating front leg lifts
- 5 rear stepping lunges on each side
- 10 2-foot mini hops
- 10 calve raises
- 5 arms circles each direction each side
- walk out into a plank, hold for 15 seconds
- lift back into a down dog stretch (walk your hand back into a bent over position with your hands and feet flat on the ground)
- walk out into a plank, hold for 15 seconds
- lift back into a down dog stretch (walk your hand back into a bent over position with your hands and feet flat on the ground)
- Lay on your back- bring your knees in and hold

SAMPLE WARM UP 2:

- Jog the room for 30 seconds
- Walking lunges slowly for 30 seconds
- Side shuffle for 30 seconds (alternate leading leg)
- Skip around room for 30 seconds
- Shadow Boxing for 30 seconds
- Walk your feet out about 3-4 feet, reach for each leg 30 seconds
- Walk your hands out into a plank with your feet wide, hold for 30 seconds
- In plank, bring your knees to your elbows, alternating sides for 30 seconds
- Lower down onto your stomach, lift your chest off the ground and slowly look over your each shoulder- 30 seconds
- Lift back up into a wide plank and reach your arms in front of you, alternating sides for 30 seconds
- Slowly stand back up and do alternating knee lifts in every direction for 30 seconds
- Squat to a leg lift, alternating sides for 30 seconds

IMPORTANCE OF BREATHING IN ALL TRAINING

"Breathing properly will improve the quality of your training."

The martial arts teach so many valuable lessons that are overlooked in other sports. One lesson that is integrated into the first stance, punch or kick that you learn is how to breathe. A comment I hear often from students is, "Why is it so hard to breathe right? Why do I keep holding my breath?" I usually answer them in saying that this means you are concentrating. It is very common that when you are extremely focused on a physical task that you often hold your breath to help quiet your mind and body in an effort to focus better. Although this happens to the best of us, you must quickly recognize how to coordinate your breath naturally with movement.

There are many examples in the martial arts where the tempo and depth of the breath in itself becomes the exercise. For example, tai chi uses breathe in a more cerebral way to improve internal health. This practice of controlled breathing contrasts the fighter that relies on the exercise of exhaling when being hit to minimize the absorption of impact.

When exercising, whether you are involved in flexibility training, general strength exercises or high intensity intervals that push you to your threshold, breathing properly will improve the quality of your training. Bottom line, oxygen facilitates movement and helps to manage your heart rate, energy and mental focus. Learning to breathe when exercising can also prevent negative physiological changes like dizziness, nausea and cramping.

Most strength training coaches will focus on having you exhale on exertion. For example, when squatting, inhale as you lower down, and exhale to stand up. Or when doing a bench press, you inhale as the bar lowers down to the chest and exhale to press the bar up. In general, this is a valuable breathing pattern for pulling and pushing movements. Additionally, it works well for counted rep style training because the movement is being done at a slow to medium pace with tremendous control. However, this pattern changes when your movement increases in speed.

If you are doing a set of jump squats for 20 seconds as fast as you can (i.e. a high intensity interval exercise), inhaling quickly every time you land and exhaling every time you jump, may cause hyperventilation. In this case, your breathing pattern should follow a natural cadence. In order to facilitate this, focus on simply keeping your mouth open and think about exhaling. If you exhale, you will naturally inhale. There are various breathing patterns that apply to high intensity training, but it would not be accurate to say you should take one breath to every 2 movements, or always cycle your breathing with every stride of your run. The speed your body is moving will completely change your breath to movement ratio. The goal is to develop a natural breathing rhythm that adjusts to all types of high intensity or power movements.

WILL MEDITATION HELP ME LEARN TO BREATH BETTER?

Meditation is truly a medicinal act for the mind and body. Although meditation is also used in various spiritual contexts, it offers physical and mental health benefits for the martial artist. Meditation has tremendous health benefits:

1. Relieves Stress
2. Helps Constipation
3. Speeds Healing
4. Can Help Cure Insomnia
5. Helps to Calm and Lessen Anxiety

More and more people are aware of these benefits since the practice of yoga and tai chi has become more widespread. Although many think of sitting with your legs crossed as the primary meditative position, there are several poses one can use in order to achieve a meditative state. One way to think of meditation is that it is a conscious relaxation.

Once you have found a comfortable position for your mediation (i.e. cross-legged position, standing or lying on your back) you can begin with breathing. Which ever position you choose, keep your back straight. Many suggest breathing through the nose. One common obstacle I hear is that they find breathing hard. It should not be a difficult act; you want to breathe without forcing your breath. Just keep breathing and use the act of exhaling as a way to relax the muscles. Many people begin by using visualization as a tool to bring them into a meditative state. Over the years, many people have shared with me the images that help them get to a meditative state: a blue sky, lying in a white room, the emotion of happiness, or their heart pumping. If you struggle even for a minute with seeing the image, it is not the right one for you. In fact, an advanced practice of mediation uses no imagery at all. This clarity will help you achieve the ideal mental state for a successful meditation.

Whether you use an image or not to begin a meditation, you must focus on your breathing. By focusing on your breathing, you will begin to dismiss distractions that prevent you from clearing your mind. You should find that after numerous breathes your mind will begin to clear and the distractions will slowly float away and you will enter into a meditative state. There are three basic breathing techniques:

1. Inhale and exhale deeply through your nose.
2. Inhale deeply through your nose and exhale slowly through your mouth.
3. Inhale deeply through your mouth and exhale slowly through your mouth.

Whichever breathing technique feels comfortable, stick to it for the 3-10 minutes you have set aside for your meditation. Although you can experiment with different breathing techniques, I suggest trying them out during separate meditation sessions, and not in one session.

PART III

EXERCISES

BODY WEIGHT EXERCISES

Decline Push-ups, Starting Position

A decline push-up can be done with your feet on any raised object. The higher your feet, the more challenging the push-up. Firmly place your feet on a chair or bench. Extend your body into a plank. Your hands should be placed directly beneath your shoulder joints. Keep your spine straight and look out in front of you.

If you want to intensify this exercise you can add a side knee to the plank. I love this variation for combat sports training because it engages many of the core muscles used in kicks and knee strikes.

Decline Push-ups, Lowered Position

Lower down into this push up while keeping your abs lifted. Look out in front of you during the entire movement.

Pull-ups

There are so many variations of pull-ups. There are also many clever ways to build your pull-up skills. A common tool is an extra thick or wide resistance band that hooks over the handles and provides support or a spot (see picture). If you are able to do pull-ups and would like to progress the challenge, you can add various core movements like knee tucks (see picture). You can also change your grip. The basic grips are wide and narrow. But you can also change the style by placing your hands in an under-hand and over-hand position.

Whichever style or variation you prefer; all pull-ups need to equally use the muscles on both sides of your body. If you are very right-side dominant, you may find that you over-compensate with the muscles on the right side when you are at a state of fatigue. I mention this, because this can quickly lead to chronic problems in the shoulder, neck and trapezius muscles. When you are lowering yourself down make sure you are in control of the movement.

Throughout the pull-up you will need to engage your abs and use your breath to help lift your body up. But the best rule of pull-ups is: feel comfortable asking for a spot.

Assisted Pull-ups

Pull-ups with Abs Twist

Pull-ups with Tight Grip

Assisted Dips

Begin by sitting on the chair or bench that you are using. Walk your feet out and shift your hips off the chair. Extend or straighten your arms to hold yourself up. Your grip on the chair should be strong and comfortable for your wrists. Make sure there is no opportunity to slip off. If it is challenging to hold yourself up, modify the position by bending your knees. Otherwise, extend your legs in front of you. For an additional challenge, lift one knee up. This requires more strength and balance.

Lower your body towards the floor by bending your elbows. You will hold the position you chose to start from when lowering your body. Then return to the starting position. Make sure when lowering your body you do not feel any discomfort in the shoulder joint. If you do, modify your range of motion.

THE BOSU BALANCE TRAINER

Using a BOSU™ Balance Trainer as part of your workout will enhance the strength of your core and your joints. BOSU, which stands for '*both sides utilized*', is a tool that also enhances balance. It was originally introduced in 1999 to a small group of Olympic teams. Because it offered unique ways to enhance balance and proprioception on a sport specific level, it received quick acceptance by the strength and conditioning community. Although there are several pieces of balance training equipment on the market, a BOSU provides the safe combination of balance training with the capabilities of performing dynamic movement. In many ways, the addition of the BOSU to the fitness community initiated the functional training movement. Below you will see a handful of exercises that will offer the average martial artist tremendous value. Before using the BOSU you should review the training tips.

1. Make sure the BOSU it is not wet or slippery. Keep it completely dry.
2. Before trying any dynamic exercises (those with movement) or single leg exercises, practice balancing on two feet. You can add simple head movements to a two-foot balance to warm up and prepare for more of a challenge.
3. Avoid falling off the BOSU. If you are losing your balance in the middle of an exercise, it is better to stop and take a controlled step off the BOSU.
4. Every exercise you do from a standing position on the BOSU requires your entire core to be engaged and knees slightly bent.
5. It is ideal to add visual tracking exercises to your warm up. When standing on the BOSU, try following your fingertips as you move them in a control manner over your head, below your head and from side to side.

Basic Crunch, Starting Position

Lie back onto the BOSU. Place the center circle in the middle of your back. If you find this to be uncomfortable, then make adjustments so you are balanced and your back feels supported. Place your feet on the ground and your hands behind your head. Open your elbows out to the side when placing them behind your head.

Basic Crunch, Position 2

Lift your upper body off the BOSU. You will notice that I added a leg lift to create more of a challenge. This is optional. To create stability, press the small of your back into the BOSU when you lift your leg and upper body.

Basic Squat, Starting Position

Stand on the BOSU. It is best to place your feet equidistant from the center circle on the BOSU. You can stand with your hands on your hips.

Basic Squat, Position 2

Bend your knees and lower your body down by sitting your weight back as if to sit in a chair. Length your arms out in front of you when squatting to assist with balance.

Clap Push-Ups

Lift your body up into a plank, placing your hands on the BOSU instead of the ground. Spread your fingers wide to utilize your entire hand. Your body will be at a slight incline. Lower down into a push-up and then burst up and off the BOSU. When you are in the air, clap your hands. When returning to the BOSU, bend your arms and return into the lower position. It is not necessary to stop in a fully extended plank. To build your skills you should practice with your knees on the ground.

Kicks on the BOSU

When kicking on the BOSU, your movement will be slow and controlled. The goal is to improve strength and stability specific to kicking, including the connective tissue in the legs. As mentioned in earlier sections, progressions can come in the form of environment changes and stability training is most successful by creating a position of safe instability.

Whichever kick you choose to begin practicing, make sure your balancing leg is placed in the center (or bulls eye) of the BOSU. Also, place the foot in the correct position. For example, a side-kick requires the basing foot to be turned out. There should also be a slight bend in your knee.

Immediately engage your guard so that your arms are assisting with your balance. You will see in the pictures that I am performing roundhouses and side-kicks. I suggest training all phases of the kicks. The chambering and re-coiling mechanics are just as important to practice as the kick itself.

This sport specific series on the BOSU is great to insert into any section of your workout. It is also a great complement to any strength workout. It can be combined with your martial arts practice or as injury prevention for weak ankles or knees.

BOSU Side Bounding

Begin with one foot on the center of the BOSU and the other directly to the side of the BOSU. Sit into a squat with your weight back into your heels

In order to bound over to the other side, jump up and over at the same time. You will land on the other side of the BOSU. When you land, the opposite foot will be on top of the BOSU on the bulls-eye. Allow your arms to swing naturally to give you momentum. Always land by bending your knees. When doing many consecutive repetitions, it is important to also develop a rhythm to maximize the benefits of this exercise.

CORE AND ABS

Bird Dog, Position 1

Start on your hands and knees. Place them directly under your shoulder joints and hips joints respectively. Lift your abdominal wall up towards your spine without holding your breath.

Bird Dog, Position 2

Lift and extend one arm and then the opposite leg. As you do this, lengthen them away from your torso, instead of lifting them up towards the ceiling. It is important to avoid any sagging in the lower back. As you lower your limbs to the ground, keep your hips and shoulders stable. Hold each arm and leg lift for about one second before changing sides.

Bicycle Crunch

Begin lying flat on your back. Your hands should be behind your head with the elbows pointing out to the side and parallel to the ground. Extend one leg and lift the opposite knee in towards your chest. Press your lower back into the floor. Lift your upper back off the floor while maintaining the position of your hands behind your head.

Rotate your torso, bringing your right knee and left shoulder towards each other. Extend your leg away from your body at an angle that does not compromise your lower back. If this is challenging, do not extend the leg completely. Alternate sides. As you perform more reps, avoid pulling on your neck. If you are unable to maintain control, do fewer reps in each set, but more sets in each workout.

Back Extension with Rotation, Position 1

Lie on your stomach placing your forehead comfortably on the back of your hands. Although you are lying on your belly, lift your abdominals up towards your spine without causing a pelvic tilt.

Back Extension with Rotation, Position 2

Raise only your head, shoulders and chest off the mat. Rotate the upper body to the right, peaking to the right. It is not necessary to lift up high from the ground in order to benefit from this exercise. Return to the starting position before rotating to the other side. Try to keep the muscles in the lower half of your body relaxed.

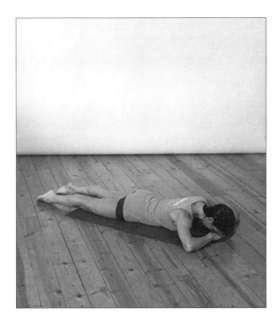

Toe Dips (Single and Double Leg)

Begin by lying on your back with your upper body relaxed and neck long. Lift your legs up together and bend them so they create a shelf-like position or 90 angle at your knees. Place your hands on the side of your body with your palms flat on the ground.

Engage your abdominals and pull them in towards your spine. Press your lower back into the floor. You can either lower one or both feet towards the floor. You must maintain the right angle at the knee in order to fully benefit from this exercise. Avoid holding your breath when lowering your foot. If you need to modify this exercise, you can lower your foot half way. If you want to challenge yourself further, then lift your head and shoulders performing a crunch in-between lowering both feet to the floor.

Prone Position- T Flaps and Y Flaps, Position 1 for the T

Although this exercise can be done on a bench lying flat on your stomach, it is being performed lying prone (on your stomach) on the floor. You can do this with or without weights. When using weights, it is recommended to use very light dumbbells (1-3 lbs).

When lying face down, extend your arms directly out to the side. Your arms should form the capital letter 'T.' The palms should face the floor. Before beginning, squeeze (or retract) your shoulder blades together.

Prone T Flaps, Position 2

Slowly lift your arms off the floor. Keep your arms straight when lifting. Continue to relax your neck and shoulders when doing this exercise. Lower the arms back to the floor. After completely a set, position your arms for the 'Ys.'

Prone Y Flaps, Position 1

The body will remain in the same position for the 'Y' Flaps. Place your arms overhead so they form a Y-shape. The exact angle of this position will be different from person to person. The palms will face towards the center of the body once they are extended fully.

Prone Y Flaps, Position 2

Lift the arms off the ground, without compromising your body position. Continue to keep the shoulder blades squeezed together while relaxing your neck. Lower to the ground.

V-Sit Position 1

This advanced core exercise should not be done if you have lower back pain. Begin in a seated position on the floor leaning back onto your hands and lift your legs slightly off the floor. Lengthen your spine. Lift your knees up off the ground, pulling them into your chest. Avoid rounding forward during this exercise. Hold this 'V' position for a second before extending your legs in front of your body.

V-Sit Position 2

Extend your legs from the 'V' sit. Even if you cannot fully straighten your legs, you should try this progression. There are several other progressions from this position. You can hold the full 'V' sit for longer periods of time or let go of the ground all together and bring your hands up into front of your face.

Single Leg Pike, Position 1

Begin by lying flat on the floor. Fully extend your arms and legs. Keep your neck relaxed.

Single Leg Pike, Position 2

Simultaneously lift your upper body and arms towards one leg. They should meet in the middle. The leg that remains on the floor should be engaged pressing down into the floor to create a connection to the ground. As you sit up, lengthen your spine and avoid rounding forward. Perform this core flexion to your level of flexibility. If you experience lower back pain or need a modification, bend the basing leg.

Forearm Planks or Alligator Plank

Although a plank can be done with your arms extended, most find it easier to do it on their forearms. When placing your forearms under your body, make sure your elbows are under the shoulder joints. Keep your forearms parallel to each other. As you lift your body up into the plank position, engage all the muscles in your core to stabilize your back. It is best to begin with your legs together.

You can add a progression to your plank by lifting your knee up towards your shoulder. I call this an alligator plank. When doing this you will be engaging the muscles along the side of your torso as well. Do not compromise your plank form when adding any progressions.

Side Plank

Place your elbow directly under your shoulder before lifting your body up into a side plank. Your body position should almost be perpendicular to the floor once it is in position. Your legs should be stacked on top of each other. Focus on maintaining your balance by engaging the muscles in your core and squeezing your inner thighs together. If you fatigue quickly and feel strain in your lower back, you can lower one leg down to the ground. Once you are in the position, look out in front of you.

DUMBBELL EXERCISES

Arnold Shoulder Press, Starting Position

This can be done from a standing or sitting position. While maintaining strong posture, hold two dumbbells in front of you the height of your chest with your palms facing your body and your elbows bent.

Arnold Shoulder Press, Ending Position

Raise the dumbbells as you rotate the palms of your hands until they are facing forward. Continue lifting the dumbbells until your arms are extended above you. Then lower the dumbbells to the original position by rotating the palms of your hands towards you.

Bent-over Row, Starting Position

Separate your feet shoulder-width apart. Your knees will remain comfortably bent throughout this exercise. While keeping your lower back flat and straight, hinge forward at the waist. A 45-degree angle from the ground is an ideal amount of forward flexion. Look out in front of you. Grip your dumbbells (this can easily be replaced with a barbell), lining your wrists up with the crease of your shoulder joint. Once the weights are firmly in your hands, retract your shoulder blades and lengthen your neck.

Bent-over Row, Ending Position

Bring the dumbbell up towards your underarm- in a rowing fashion. As the dumbbell rows, squeeze the shoulder blades together. You can lift both weights simultaneously or perform one row at a time. Avoid rounding forward while doing this motion. Lower the dumbbell with control and repeat the action.

Hammer Bicep Curl, Starting Position

Begin by standing up straight with good posture. Slightly bend your knees. This can also be performed from a seated position. Place your arms with the weights along the side of your body with your palms facing your legs.

Hammer Bicep Curl, Ending Position

While keeping your elbows close to your torso, curl the weights up towards your shoulder joint. Slowly return the weights to the starting position.

Side Raises

Side raises with dumbbells can be performed while seated or standing. Here they are shown from the side plank position. Make sure if you are seated, that your feet are flat on the ground. I prefer side raises with the palms forward. They can also be down with the palms down.

The dumbbells will begin at your sides. Lift the dumbbells without changing your posture. Avoid lifting your shoulders to lift your arms. Do not lift your hands higher than your chin.

Plank Dumbbell Row with Rotation and Shoulder Press, Starting Position

Lower your body into a push-up plank. Your body should be parallel to the ground with your feet separated about 2-3 feet. Engage your core and keep your abs lifted up towards your spine. Place your hand on the dumbbell that is on the ground. Place the other hand flat and firm onto the floor.

Plank Dumbbell Row with Rotation and Shoulder Press, Rowing Position

Row one dumbbell up towards the crease of your underarm. Continue to look out in front of your body throughout the exercise in order to maintain correct spinal alignment.

Plank Dumbbell Row with Rotation and Shoulder Press, Rotation Position

From the row, rotate your body into a side plank position. Allow your hips to naturally follow this action. The body will be perpendicular to the ground. To assist with establishing a strong side plank, press the floor away from your body as you lift your side body away from the floor. During the rotation, load the dumbbell comfortably on the side of your chest. Your gaze will change to look up towards the ceiling.

While holding your side plank, press the dumbbell straight up towards the ceiling. Make sure the press is directly above your shoulder joint. Lift your side body up towards the ceiling. Reverse your movement with control. You can isolate one side or switch sides every rep.

Step-ups with Dumbbells

There are several types of surfaces you can use for step-ups. They can be done on various types of boxes or stepping tools. The height of the box should cause a 90-degree angle. If the step height is too high, it may lead to lower back problems and various types of compensations.

Begin with the dumbbells by your side and your foot firmly placed on the step. As you step up, engage your abs and keep your shoulders stacked over your hips. Avoid bending forward. If you look up as you step, it will assist with maintaining this alignment and overall balance.

Carefully lower down, placing your free foot firmly on the ground. You can repeat the step up on one side or alternative legs.

Lunges

There are many variations of a lunge. The muscular involvement of a lunge is perfect. It involves large muscles groups, integrates the core and develops balance. It can be modified for new comers and easily progressed. It can be programmed for maximum load strength training or adapted into a plyometric. Additionally, lunges can be done in any exercise setting. It is for these reasons that the lunge is used in many of the programs in this book. Below are a handful of variations that are ideal for any martial arts program.

Front Stepping Lunge – Two Options: Forward Stepping or Off-Angle, Starting Position

Stand with your feet hip-width apart. Your hands can go on your hips or use them to hold your dumbbells. Relax your shoulders and keep your posture lifted and core engaged.

Front Stepping Lunge –Two Options: Forward Stepping or Off-Angle, Position 2

Whether you choose to step off-angle or straight forward, you must control the length of the step. When taking either step, avoid hinging forward from the hips. Remain in control of your posture so that when you land, your weight is in the proper place in your foot. The length of the stride should be almost two strides of your natural gait.

Front Stepping Lunge – Two Options: Forward Stepping or Off-Angle, Position 3

Lower down into both legs. Keep your weight centered between both legs so that you are completely balanced. You should have a 90-degree angle at your knees and hip. This would provide you with the ideal alignment. If you are performing an off angle lunge, you will find the rear leg to be more extended (it requires more balance and flexibility).

DYNAMIC FLEXIBILITY EXERCISES

As mentioned earlier, dynamic flexibility exercises are an ideal way to thoroughly prepare the body for any type of workout. Since modern martial arts are dynamic in nature, it is best to include a handful of exercises that increase blood flow and mobility to the joints in every training session. Here are a few exercises that I rely on when doing strength, conditioning, and martial arts workouts.

Arm Circles are a simple exercise that most of us have done since PE in grammar school. Arm circles should always be performed at a speed where you have complete control. The circular action of the arm should be done forward and backward. Similar to the backstroke and free-style swim, this movement allows the arm to move through the shoulder joint. Your torso should also rotate naturally. Make sure you stay within your range of motion. You can perform this exercise with your palm either turned in or out.

Leg Lifts can be done in a few different ways. You should begin with the hips and shoulders square with one another. As you lift your leg, you must first completely shift your weight onto your basing leg. This dynamic stretch is one of my favorites because is also builds strength and stability in the basing leg. Engage your abs every time you lift your leg for a controlled leg swing. I suggest flexing your foot to promote a deeper stretch behind the calf and knee. Begin lifting the leg directly in front of your body so it lines up with the mid-line of your body. Make sure you control the lowering of the leg each time.

A great variation on the basic leg lift is one that moves across the body and adds trunk rotation. I suggest opening your arms to the side and lifting the leg towards the opposite hand while rotating your upper body towards the side of the leg being lifted. Keep your foot flexed.

Hip Openers are very common in martial arts. Lift your leg and bend it in half. Circle the leg from the inside of the body towards the outside of the body. Keep your hips and shoulders square. The goal is to move completely through the hip joint.

PLYOMETRICS

Box Jumps are a standard plyometric exercise. They build tremendous strength in the legs. There are also many progressions. There are a few safety tips for this exercise. Make sure the box or surface you are jumping on is secure and stable. I suggest you step off the box to return to your beginning position instead of jumping backwards.

Begin in a shoulder to hip-width stance. Bend your knees to begin your jump and bend your knees when you land. As you begin your jump, look up and allow your arms to swing naturally with the movement.

When you land on your box, bend your knees and continue to engage your abs. Avoid looking at your feet. To repeat the exercise, step off the box.

Hamstring Curl Jump is a great explosive exercise for building martial arts skills. This exercise begins from an athletic stance, with your feet shoulder-width apart. Bend your knees and allow your arms to naturally move with your body. Then jump straight up.

When you are in the air, fold your legs behind you. As they unfold, you return to the ground with your knees bent.

Pop Ups are an excellent sport-specific exercise for martial artists. It has great sport-specific application.

Begin on your stomach as if you have just lowered down from a push up. Shift some of your body weight onto the balls of your feet and place your palms directly under your shoulder joints. While inhaling, burst up by lifting your hips towards the ceiling.

As you explosively lift your hips up towards the ceiling, slide your feet underneath your body. It is best to do this by pushing off of your hands and feet at the same time.

Once your feet are under your body, firmly place them on the ground.

Once you have created a stable position, your hands move immediately off the floor into your guard. The final position is a fighting stance. To repeat this exercise, reverse your movement.

Sprawl to a Jump Tuck is an advanced explosive drill. It can be modified in many ways. You can eliminate the jump or the sprawl action to simplify this exercise. If you are uncertain how to properly sprawl, you can replace the sprawl with a plank position.

Begin and finish in a fighting stance. This plyometric drill can keep you in the context of your martial arts stance. During all phases of this drill, keep your gaze up.

As you lower down into the sprawl, bend your knees to lower yourself to the ground. This movement requires both the knees and hips to bend simultaneously. Avoid hinging forward and leading with your head. Once you have lowered your body down to the ground, place your hands directly under your shoulders. I call this the transitional position.

Sprawl or shoot your legs behind you. Separate your legs. It is optional to lower one hip to the ground. If you are modifying this portion of the exercise, extend your legs back into a wide plank. In either case, the balls of your feet should remain connected to the ground. Then, reverse yourself back through the transitional position by lifting your hips up towards the ceiling and sliding your feet underneath you.

As you move through the transitional position, you will stand up building momentum to assist you with bursting into the jump. Your hands should travel with you. Keep looking up during this movement. As you jump, tuck your knees under your arms. Remember to bend your knees and return to your fighting stance as you land. If you are fatiguing or new to this exercise, just skip this step and repeat the first 3 phases of the movement. If you have a wrestling background or you are familiar with the sprawl as a defensive technique for takedowns, make adjustments to suit your style. This will offer a realistic application of the drill, and ultimately improve your martial arts skills.

SUSPENSION STRAP TRAINING

There are many brands of suspension training straps. It is one of the most innovative additions to the strength and conditioning world. This tool forces the exerciser to utilize his or her bodyweight to perform a wide range of functional and conventional exercises. Although there are ways to add weights to some of the exercises, it is best to learn how to manipulate your body angle and positions to increase the intensity. Other than building strength and endurance, suspension strap exercises also integrate stability training.

Suspension trainers are affordable. You can adjust the length of the straps to the height of the user or the space you have available. Utilize the wide range of free videos online for proper anchoring methods, whether you are using them at home, work or inside of your school. In many cases, you will need to invest into a proper anchoring system so that the strap is fixed and able to handle your body weight.

Standing Bicep Curl

Begin by leaning back at an appropriate angle while holding onto the straps. Engage your upper back muscles. Squeeze your shoulder blades together and relax your neck. Straighten your arms and tighten your abs. Place your arms out in front of you at the height of your shoulders with the palms facing up.

Once you are in position, bend the arms at the elbows simultaneously. Maintain the same posture as your beginning position throughout the exercise. As you curl, your arms do not move. They will remain parallel to the ground. Return to your beginning position.

Body Weight Rows - 3 variations

The body weight row is a staple exercise on the suspension straps. There are many variations. All of them offer great core training. You can begin by leaning back with your legs extended while holding onto the straps. If you squeeze a roller or towel between your knees, you will integrate more of the muscles in your legs and core (this is optional). Make sure your upper back muscles are engaged. Squeezing your shoulder blades and relaxing your neck will help you maintain good posture. If this position is difficult for you, modify by bending your knees (I refer to this as a table-top). The last variation I would like to suggest is to increase the intensity by simply lifting one knee up towards your chest while performing the exercise.

While engaging the muscles in your upper back, row your body up towards the strap handles. Look up at the straps as you row. If you are beginning from a table-top position, lift your chest up as you row. You can use your legs to assist you with the exercise. If you are performing the more challenging version with the leg lift, then kick your leg out when you reach the top of the row.

Hamstring Curls from a Bridge

Lie flat on your back and place your feet in the soft end of the straps. Extend your legs (without locking your knees). You can place your hands on the side of your body to assist with balance. Lift your hips while flattening your abs. Stabilize your body in this position.

Pull your heels towards your glutes by bending your knees. Your hips remain elevated while performing this curl action. Then return your legs to the extended position and repeat the curl for the entire set. If holding this elevated plank is challenging, you can lower your hips to the floor between each repetition.

Standing Chest Fly

Adjust the straps to a length that offers you the appropriate challenge. The angle of your body in relation to the ground will also determine the level of difficulty. The more upright your body is positioned, the easier the exercise will be. If you would like to increase the intensity, lengthen the straps to bring your body closer to the ground. Place the straps in your hands and keep your legs extended. The handles should line up with your shoulder joints and your feet should connect you to the floor by the balls-of-your-feet. Engage all the muscles in your core so your body moves as one solid unit.

As you lower your body towards the floor, open your arms out to the side. Keep your elbows slightly bent as you open your arms. The wider your arms, the more challenging this exercise. Continue to engage the muscles in your core and look out in front of you as you perform this exercise. Use your abs to assist you with returning back to the starting position. Press the palms together as you return back to the starting plank position.

Single Leg Squats

There are several versions of the single leg squat. This version places less pressure on the knee. Position yourself on one leg. Keep your back straight and look up. Shift your weight into the center of your foot and the heel. As you sit down, avoid shifting your weight too far forward. Do not sit lower than a 90 degree angle. In order to maximize the benefits of this exercise, control how much you use your upper body during the squat. The straps are intended to offer assistance with your balance, not pull you up.

Tricep Press

Reach your arms overhead and grab the straps. Pull your elbows in close to your head and carefully walk your feet behind you. This will create a position where you are leaning forward. In order to remain balanced and strong in your core, hold a neutral pelvis and engage your glutes. Allow your heels to rise slightly off the ground.

As you extend your arms, you will move your body. The goal is to maintain your body position as you straighten your arms. Then bend the elbows to repeat the exercise.

Push-ups and Planks

The value of push-ups and planks is their ability to adapt to so many training settings. When using the strap, place your feet in the straps and walk your hands out in front of you. You can shorten your straps to place more weight in your upper body. Your hands should be located directly under your shoulder joints. Then proceed to a hold, and move into a push up or begin alternating your knees for knee tucks. You can combine all these elements while in this position. For all positions, keep your spine straight, your head held up and your abs engaged.

CABLE MACHINES

It is ideal to use a cable machine that has an adjustable head because you can change the height of the cable cart. Although I find value in using conventional dumbbells, barbells and plate-loaded machines, I personally enjoy weight training from a cable machine the most because it can be adapted to specific movements and forces the muscles of the core to be involved. Once you have surveyed the various types of attachments that the machine has, you can then choose which exercises in this chapter are most appropriate for your workout.

Tips:

- Make sure the attachment you pick is appropriate for the exercise(s) you have chosen.
- Make sure the pin on the cable cart is fully locked into the frame of the machine.
- Make sure you have completely pushed the pin into the hole of the weight stack.
- Adjust the cable cart to fit your body. Most of these exercises are intended to be specific to your personal height.
- Always set up your body in a position where the cable in slightly off the stack. You want to avoid the weight from clanking as you return it to your Starting Position.
- When doing these exercises, look in front of you. Avoid looking down. An upward gaze will assist in maintaining good posture throughout all the movements.

Sport Specific Strengthening Using an Adjustable Cable Machine

Most of the exercises included in this section are considered to be sport specific to the martial arts. They are intended to heighten muscle awareness and build strength. You should never compromise the technique of the martial movement in order to increase the weight. These exercises will also help to reinforce technique and make you more aware of the muscles involved to properly generate power. The return of the weight to the Starting Position is always the trickiest. During this phase of the exercise action, you will perform it with control. Do not allow the cable pulley to whip or snap your leg, or arm back into the Starting Position. It is during this phase that you are enhancing joint stability and strengthening the connective tissue. I have always used these exercises to heighten my awareness of the muscular involvement, therefore making my fundamentals like punching and kicking stronger. The speed of all these exercises is slow and controlled.

Cable Lead Jab 1 (Straight Punches)

Line the cable cart up above your shoulder. Then position your body in your fighting stance with the cable on the outside of your shoulder (any other placement will cause the cable to hit your body). Before extending the arm, make sure you are centered in your stance. This exercise is not intended to involve hip flexion or forward hinging from the waist. This will also serve as the re-set or re-coil position after each extension.

Cable Lead Jab 2

The extension of the punch requires you to maintain your stance. As you extend the cable, do so in a straight line. Avoid lifting your elbow to the side on the extension. To gain full range and length of the punch, allow your torso to naturally rotate and extend your arm forward.

Cable Cross Jab 1 (Straight Punches)

Line the cable cart up above your shoulder. Then position your body in your fighting stance with the cable on the outside of your body. Keep your elbows down along your body in a guard position. Maintain the proper center of gravity for your stance. Before extending the cable, make sure you keep weight in your rear leg.

Cable Cross Jab 2

As you perform this straight cross-punch, you will initiate the extension from the legs. Begin pivoting from your rear foot. Extend the arm with the cable without transferring all your weight to the front leg. Be mindful of proper technique. Control your weight when rotating your torso on the pivot. Return the cable to your guard (position 1). Avoid lifting your elbow.

Cable Rear / Power Uppercut 1

Begin with the cable cart in the lowest position. Begin in your fighting stance. Keep your lead arm in a tight guard. Hold the cable in a position that does not compromise your fighting stance.

Cable Rear / Power Uppercut 2

Begin by pivoting your rear foot and rotating your torso. Your knees should bend slightly to access the power from the rear leg. When moving into the uppercut, keep the arm close to the body. The punch will move up while the torso continues to rotate and the foot will pivot. At the end of the uppercut, avoid transferring all your weight onto your front leg. Return to your Starting Position.

Cable Knee Strike Rear Leg 1

You will need an ankle strap for this exercise. Begin with the cable cart in the lowest position. Line your hip and leg up directly in front of the cable. Begin in a fighting stance. Like in Muay Thai, it is best for the rear foot to be on the ball of the foot. Avoid being flat-footed during this exercise because it will cause you to lose your balance and interfere with maximizing the benefits of the exercise.

Cable Knee Strike rear Leg 2

As you move the knee up through this strike, be mindful of your balance. As with all knee strikes, engage the muscles in your buttocks (gluts) as you lift and bend the knee. The knee bends completely and the foot should point down. Engage your abdominals while throwing this controlled knee. Although Thai stylists often rise up on the basing leg for this strike, it is better to remain grounded. Keep your hands in an active guard and your base leg bent. Return to your Starting Position with control, like all cable exercises.

Abduction Lift for Side and Roundhouse 1

Set the height of the cable where you can easily hold your leg up in a side leg lift. Before beginning, it is critical that you first gauge your range of motion. You will begin this exercise with your leg lifted and suspended in a sidekick or roundhouse extension. The ankle, knee, hip and shoulder should all be in a straight line. Avoid hinging forward at the hips. Introduce yourself to this exercise with very little weight. Place the pin in the weight stack, and then place the cuff attachment on the exercising leg.

Once you have comfortably placed the ankle strap on your leg, carefully walk away from the weight stack, keeping weight on the exercising leg to avoid the weight whipping your leg off the ground. Once you are far enough away from the weight stack, allow your leg to gently rise up. Keep in mind, this exercise is advanced and requires tremendous balance. In order to avoid struggling with your balance, you can use a chair to help you maintain perfect form. Position your base foot so that it faces away from the cable machine. Once your foot is externally rotated, bring your hands up and engage your core.

Slowly allow your leg to lift. It will be slightly lower than the cable head height. Engage your core and begin contracting your glutes. This exercise requires your gluteal to be engaged to ensure the correct muscular contractions.

Abduction Lift for Side and Roundhouse 2

Whether you are using a chair or not to balance, maintain proper kicking posture. As you lower your leg, squeeze your inner thighs together. This action of adduction will build strength in the working leg and the basing leg. Carefully return your leg to the beginning position. Avoid the cable whipping your leg back up to the Starting Position. I suggest doing all your sets on one leg before switching sides.

Bicep Curls Kneeling and Rear Facing, Starting Position

Begin by facing away from the machine and kneel down. Keep in mind that you can easily do this from a standing position with your feet neutral. Both positions require good posture with your shoulders relaxed, neck long and shoulder blades pulled back (retracted).

If you experience any discomfort in your knees from kneeling, you should perform this exercise from a comfortable standing position. I chose to do it from the kneeling position because it requires more core strength.

Adjust the cable to the lowest position on the machine. If are using a cable machine that also has adjustable arms (like the one in the picture), make sure they are not too wide. Bicep curls on a cable machine work with several different types of attachments. You can also isolate one arm at a time or curl both arms simultaneously. This is another variation of the exercise. This version of a kneeling bicep curl develops core and shoulder stability and strength.

Once you are in a stable Starting Position, bring your elbows along the side of your body. Make sure you do not feel any strain in your shoulder joint.

Bicep Curl Kneeling and Facing Away, Ending Position

Begin by either curling the handles towards your shoulder or until you can achieve complete flexion of the elbow. When curling, keep your elbows along the side of your body and your handgrip strong around the handles. Avoid bending at your wrist to complete your curl or hunching forward in your posture. Slowly return the handle to the Starting Position, keeping your torso steady throughout every repetition.

High Bicep Curl Kneeling and Facing Machine, Starting Position

Place the cable heads in the high position. If you experience any discomfort in your knees from kneeling, you should perform this exercise from a comfortable standing position. You will accomplish the same bicep muscle recruitment whether you are standing or kneeling. The kneeling position adds more core strength and stability to the overall exercise. Once you are in a comfortable Starting Position, extend your arms in front of you. The position of the handles will be above your head. Before beginning your curl, keep your shoulders lowered, neck long and shoulder blades drawn back (retracted). Your posture is slightly shifted back, which will force you to also engage the muscles in your lower back (extensors) that assist with stabilizing the exercise.

High Bicep Curl Kneeling and Facing Machine, Ending Position

As you begin to curl the handles towards your shoulders, the bottom of your arms (triceps) will be parallel to the ground and the elbows will be in line with your shoulder joints. When performing this high curl, maintain this position throughout each repetition. Avoid lowering your arms when you curl.

Standing Chest Fly, Starting Position

Adjust the height of the cable heads so that they are above your shoulders. If you are using a cable machine with adjustable arms (like the one in the picture), open the width to about a 45-degree angle. The cable arms need to be on the outside of your body. Step forward with each handle and place your body into a staggered stance like the picture. Make sure you have good posture, relax your shoulders and lengthen your neck. Your upper body should be positioned slightly in front of your hips. Your hips and shoulders should be square with each other and the cables should be pulled off the stack to line up with your shoulder joints.

The Starting Position of the handle should have all the joints of the arm in a straight line (reference my right arm in the picture). Engage your core to help maintain this ideal posture. Although I am doing this chest fly with both arms, this exercise can be executed with one arm at a time. The Starting Position will be the same whether you do this with one or two arms.

Standing Chest Fly, Ending Position

As you close your arms, make sure you maintain your starting posture. Close your arms towards the midline of your body. The arms should line up with your chest. Your palms will face each other at the end of the movement. Depending on the mobility of your shoulder joint, you may need to shorten your range. If you have limitations in your shoulder movement, make adjustments to train pain-free or choose another exercise.

Basic High Cable Chop, Starting Position

You will only need to use one side of the cable machine for this exercise. Place the cable cart in the lowest position. Widen your feet about 24-36 inches and center your weight with your knees slightly bent. Extend your arms in front of you and place both hands on the handle. Relax your shoulders, keep your neck long and lift your posture up. Before beginning this exercise with rotation, make sure your weight is even between both legs. In this version of a high cable chop, the body is sideways to the cable machine. It is less difficult than other versions and requires less movement of the feet.

Basic High Cable Chop, Ending Position

While keeping your arms extended in front of your body, rotate your body in an upward chopping motion. In order to complete this movement, you will push off the foot closest to the cable machine and pivot. Pivot on the ball of the foot. This movement will require your arms, torso and hips to rotate towards the outside leg (see finishing pose). The arm position will be about a 45-degree angle above your head. As you do this upward chop movement, keep your shoulders down and avoid leaning forward to complete the action. Slowly control the cable as it returns to the Starting Position.

High Chop in Lunge, Starting Position

You will only need to use one side of the cable machine for this exercise. Place the cable head in the lowest position. Begin facing the machine in a split squat or lunge. Your feet should be wide enough for your knees to be at right angles. Place your weight in the center of your foot that is closest to the machine. The rear foot is connected to the floor by the ball-of-your-foot. Keep your shoulders on top of your hips. Avoid bending forward when performing this exercise.

Fully extend your arms out in front of you (without locking the elbows) and place both hands on the handle. In this version of the high chop, you will be rotating and pivoting 180-degrees, therefore facing the opposite direction.

High Chop in Lunge, Ending Position

With your arms extended in front of you, begin to rotate your body 180-degrees from your Starting Position. Both feet will pivot and turn with the body. Your hips and shoulders will continue to rotate with the entire movement. Once you have completed the entire movement, the arms will be extended slightly above your head. Maintain the lunging posture throughout the exercise.

External Rotator Cuff, Starting Position

Before beginning this exercise, roll a towel or shirt and tuck it under your arm. This will provide the necessary stability for the shoulder blade, which will promote isolation of the rotator cuff. Stand with good posture, in a sideways position. Place the cable handle in the hand furthest from the machine. Bend the arm to a 90-degree angle and place it firmly on the towel against your rib cage.

The forearm of the working arm will begin folded across your stomach. The right angle position of the arm will be parallel to the hips.

External Rotator Cuff, Ending Position

While keeping the upper arm pressed up against the towel, rotate the handle outward, away from the machine. When performing this movement, the forearm should move parallel to the ground. Full range of motion on this exercise is different for everyone. Avoid rotating your hips and shoulders with the exercise. The entire movement is generated from the shoulder joint.

Straight Arm Overhead Reach, Starting Position

Begin by facing the cable machine with the cable heads in the lowest position. Stand in a neutral shoulder-width stance, with your knees bent and perfect posture. Grab the cables and place them in the opposite hands, so they are crossed one over the other. Turn your palms down and extend your arms. Before lifting the arms, engage your upper back, make sure your shoulder blades are drawn back and your chest is lifted.

Straight Arm Overhead Reach, Ending Position

Extend your arms without bending at the wrists or elbows. Although the cables are crossed, you will be reaching directly above your body. If you experience any limitation in your shoulder's range of motion, adjust the height you lift your arms. As you are reaching, your focus should be on keeping your shoulder blades drawn down into your back. Without this effort to stabilize, you may experience a pinching sensation in the shoulder and your range of motion will be limited.

Single Arm Wide Row, Starting Position

Begin by facing the machine and adjust the arm of the machine so that the handles are about the height of your shoulders. Your feet should be in a shoulder-width stance with the knees slightly bent. Your posture should be lifted with the neck long and shoulders relaxed. When gripping the handles, turn your palms down.

Single Arm Wide Row, Ending Position

Row one arm by bending it at the elbow. The rowing motion should pull the handle back to the crease of the under arm. When executing this movement, retract your shoulder blade. Allow your gaze to follow the movement. There will be natural rotation. This additional action will involve more of the muscles in your core. As soon as you begin to return the arm to the Starting Position, begin rowing on the other side of your body. The exercise is intended to become a pulley-like movement.

Standing Rear Deltoid T-Fly, Starting Position

Begin by facing the machine and adjust the arm of the machine so that the handles are about the height of your shoulders. Your feet should be in a shoulder-width stance with the knees slightly bent. Your posture should be lifted with the neck long and shoulders relaxed. When gripping the handles, the palms will face the opposite sides of the body.

Standing Rear Deltoid T-Fly, Ending Position

Begin opening the arms to the side creating a 'T.' As the arms perform this fly, they are fully extended (without locking the elbows). As the arms reach the 'T' position, the shoulder blades squeeze together, as if to hold a pencil in place. Avoid bending the arms at the elbow.

Standing Torso Lateral Flexion, Starting Position

Line your body up with only one cable. Turn your body sideways to the cable. Place the cable cart in the lowest position. Stand in a shoulder-width stance with your knees slightly bent. Your posture should be as tall as possible while still maintaining a balanced neutral stance. Lift the handle up over the shoulder closest to the weight stack and stabilize it in that position. Stabilizing this area requires the shoulder blades to be drawn back and down. Your gaze should be in front of you. Place the free hand on your hip to assist with posture and balance.

Standing Torso Lateral Flexion, Ending Position

While holding the arm stable overhead, begin your lateral flexion or side bend. As you perform this movement, the side of body (furthest from the machine) will shorten or contract. Avoid wobbling your hips during this action. The hips and shoulders remain square with each other. Slowly return to your starting position.

Triceps Press Down, Starting Position

Begin by facing the cable machine. Place your feet no wider than your hips. Place the arms of the cable machine above your head. Sit down into your legs and slightly hinge forward. Although your upper body is hinged forward, keep your back flat. Relax the shoulders and neck.

Bend the elbows and frame them against your rib cage. Press the handles behind your body.

Triceps Press Down, Ending Position

While keeping your elbows framed against your body, press your palms down and back. Extend your arms fully during the pressing action. Squeeze your triceps for a moment at the end of this extension. As you perform each extension or press, avoid locking your elbow.

KETTLEBELLS (KB)

There is an absolute need for explosivity in martial athletics. The kettlebell is a great addition to martial arts training. The kettlebell is one tool that can quickly enhance power. It will also build strength and help with fat loss.

Your approach to adding the kettlebell into your routine must be responsible. Therefore, read through the exercises provided before adding them to your routine. Each exercise offers tips. These tips provide a framework for keeping you injury free. But in truth, all the tips provided collectively apply to each and every exercise listed. Therefore, I suggest reading the entire section before adding any of the exercises to a workout routine.

I am going to give a brief overview of safe kettlebell training and the exercises I feel complement all the variables that make up a balanced martial athlete.

According to Mike Mahler, a kettlebell training expert and respected fitness professional, it is important that your kettlebell training workout incorporates the "five pillars.":

- Press
- Pull
- Squat
- Lower body pull
- Core

I am less concerned that every time you use a kettlebell, you include exercises from each of these categories. However, I want you to choose exercises that fit with your specific goals. With each of these exercises you must use proper technique and understand how to gauge your intensity to avoid injury. I encourage you to try both a kettlebell-only workout and a workout that includes a couple kettlebell exercises in a circuit style program. The exercises I have chosen below represent each of these categories. If you start enjoying the kettlebell exercises, please read additional educational sources to expand your knowledge of kettlebell training.

General Tips:

- Look in front of you when doing all kettlebell exercises.
- Be mindful of your back and how it feels that day. Avoid kettlebell training when you are experiencing any back discomfort.
- Warm up your back, shoulders, core and legs before beginning any kettlebell lifting.
- Practice with a lighter kettlebell before using one that exceeds 35 pounds for men and 20 for women.
- The goal is to generate power from your legs when doing most kettlebell exercises. This will become more apparent once you increase your weight.
- When gripping the kettlebell, avoid flexing the wrists. The hands and wrists should be in natural alignment, similar to a punch. Be mindful of your grip especially as you increase the weight of your kettlebell.
- If you are prone to sweaty palms when you work out, it is recommended that you use chalk.
- Avoid wearing boxing wraps, MMA gloves or martial arts hand grips when you are performing kettlebell exercises.
- Relax the muscles in your face when using the kettlebell. This will prevent you from straining your neck or creating compensations in your upper back posture.
- Use your breath to assist with all the movements. Keep your mouth open to promote natural breathing.

Single Arm Swing, Starting Position

Swings are the first kettlebell exercises to learn. Place the kettlebell under the center of your body. Once in the straddle position, sit your hips back into a deep squat with your butt back, weight in your heels and your back flat. You want to maintain core strength and correct posture at all times. Your eyes should look forward while doing this exercise. Remember this is not a front raise. Place your feet in a wide squat.

Single Arm Swing, Swinging Position and Alignment

The kettlebell will begin swinging behind you to gain momentum before it travels in front of your body. The free arm will act as a counter balance and should naturally swing on its own. As you lift the kettlebell, you should access the muscles in your legs to thrust your hips forward. The combination of the swinging action, along with the explosive involvement of the legs, is the key to this exercise and most of the other kettlebell exercises described in this book. The kettlebell should swing about the height of your head. Keep your abs engaged as you return the swinging arm to the starting position and perform several repetitions. Regardless of the number of reps in your set, you will still utilize controlled momentum to avoid injuries. As the kettlebell lowers, your knees and hips will bend, allowing you to repeat the exercise.

Two Handed Swing, Starting Position

Straddle the kettlebell and align your body as you did in the one arm swing. Begin in a squat. Place both hands on the kettlebell without flexing the wrist. Since both hands are there to guide the kettlebell through the swing, you will quickly find yourself moving up in weight. However, a lightweight is ideal for learning the technique, but once you have achieved the correct form and how to apply it, a heavier weight with this exercise will force you to use your legs. It is at this point that the exercise becomes challenging. Engage your entire core so that your back does not become strained throughout this exercise. Keep your neck long and shoulders lowered down into your back.

Two Handed Swing, Swinging Position and Alignment

The actual swing will begin behind and underneath your body. The strength for this exercise comes from driving the hips forward and bursting through all the muscles in your legs.

To avoid straining your shoulders, keep your upper back muscles engaged. Make sure you are keeping your back flat and lift your abdominals inward to create a strong core. When ending your set, decrease the speed of the swing and place it on the ground softly.

Single Arm Row from Split Stance with Rotation, Starting Position

This exercise is very similar to a single arm bent over row with a dumbbell. Although there are many variations of the row, this one will begin in a split stance with your feet staggered. The width of your feet should be fairly comfortable. You should not feel any strain in your lower back from the forward flexion. Additionally, your legs need to be able to bend and straighten comfortably so that as you perform this row, the action can become dynamic.

Begin with your knees bent about 20-30 degrees. Hinge forward while keeping your back flat. The kettlebell should be placed directly under your shoulder. Firmly grip the handle of the kettlebell. Your wrist and shoulder should form a straight line.

Single Arm Row from Split Stance with Rotation, Row Position and Alignment

With a firm grip, pull the kettlebell up towards the crease of your underarm. This lifting action will require you to burst up through your legs. At the end of your row, your torso should naturally rotate towards the kettlebell. Lift your elbow up towards the ceiling during the rowing action. This row action has no swinging motion like the previous exercises described.

The free arm will act as a natural counter balance throughout this exercise. Keep it in front of your body. As you begin to lower the kettlebell back to the starting position, allow your knees to bend simultaneously with the lowering of the kettlebell. When doing a set, you do not need to return the kettlebell to the floor in-between repetitions. A succession of reps will be done with each row action, fluidly lowering and then re-rowing the kettlebell. Use the legs to create explosive energy.

Side Lunge, Starting Position (two foot positions)

Begin with your legs separated about 3-shoulder widths. Although your legs begin straight, they are not locked.

There are two-foot positions. Option A begins with your feet pointed straight head and parallel to each other. This will recruit the hamstrings, quadriceps and gluteal. Option B will begin with the feet slightly turned out (externally rotated). This starting position will recruit more of the inner thigh muscles than option A. Both versions have tremendous value for the martial artist.

Lift the kettlebell up with both hands. It will be held below your waistline. When holding the kettlebell, your shoulders should be drawn back and down. Squeeze your shoulder blades together while engaging the abdominals.

Side Lunge, Ending Position

Bend one knee while keeping the other leg straight. This exercise is very different from a split squat/lunge. This side lunge requires the upper body to slightly hinge forward by flexing at the hips. As you bend your knee and flex forward, make sure that you maintain your balance. Keep your back flat and shoulders drawn back.

As you shift your weight from side to side, you need to keep weight in both feet. It is important to keep the foot of the straight leg grounded. As you bend your leg in one direction, make sure the knee does not bend past your toes (in either direction). This example of the side lunge is stationary. You can shift from side to side, transitioning through the starting position. Or, you can isolate one side and do a set in one direction before moving to the other side. In either case, the kettlebell is being used as weight and there is no dynamic element in moving the kettlebell. The kettlebell remains in the center of your body throughout this exercise.

The depth of the side lunge should be comfortable. Remember that you need to be able to lift dynamically out of the lunge. Your range of motion in this exercise is based upon your flexibility.

A   B

Snatch and Press, Starting Position for Swing

The snatch is an ideal exercise for developing explosive power. This is an advanced exercise. Try it once you have become comfortable with swings. The starting position is the same as the swing. The kettlebell is placed slightly behind you and you approach the kettlebell through your deep squat, sitting your butt back and keeping your back flat. Keep your elbow softly bent during this exercise.

Snatch and Press, Position 2 of the Swing into the Snatch

This movement begins by swinging the kettlebell from between your legs. You must have tremendous control over the momentum behind the swing when flipping the kettlebell. The kettlebell begins to flip when it travels past your chest. Even a controlled flip will result in the kettlebell resting on the back of your hand. This occurs while in the standing position. If you find the "flip-action" challenging, seek out one of the many free online videos of this technique to clarify the movement.

Snatch and Press, Position of Body at the End of the Snatch

The driving force of the hips facilitates this flip. It is a completely fluid action. There is no pause in this exercise until you reach this portion of the movement.

Use the free arm as a counter balance and allow it to naturally assist with balance as the kettlebell is pressed above the body (directly above the shoulder joint).

Snatch and Press, Lowering the Kettlebell

Lower down into a half squat while catching the kettlebell. Although it is not necessary to lower into a squat, I prefer the wider stance for martial arts. Naturally, this option does continue to keep the legs involved in every phase of this exercise.

As the kettlebell lowers down, it is slightly in front of the shoulder and the elbow remains comfortably flexed. To maximize control over the kettlebell, maintain good posture. Avoid rounding forward during this action. The next phase will have you reverse this entire motion.

Snatch and Press, Pressing Posture

Burst back up into a press. Drive from your legs as you lift the kettlebell overhead. Continue to use your free arm to assist with balance. It should aid in keeping the rhythm of the movement fluid. Although the picture makes it seem like you are pausing at the top of the press, this motion is seamless with the kettlebell action when it flips back to the returning position.

Snatch and Press, Flip from the Press to the Swing

The kettlebell makes its flip back as it passes in front of your face during the downward portion of the swing. The flip happens with the elbow softly bent. During the flip, the handle loosens to allow the flip of the kettlebell and then re-grips firmly to control the swing until the arm begins to decelerate.

Snatch and Press, Ending Position

The final position is exactly where you began. Like all phases of this exercise, the movement is fluid. Considering this is done for many reps, you will allow the end of the swing to lower your body into a solid squat where you have absolute control of your posture. In order to begin the next rep, you will burst from your legs again, driving your hips forward and exploding up into the snatch portion of the exercise.

Sit-Up, Starting Position

Lay flat on your mat with your legs fully extended. Hold your kettlebell with two hands directly above your chest. Although you are lying down, engage your upper back the same way you would in any standing exercise. Keep your arms lengthened and your neck long.

Sit-Up, Transition Position

Begin to sit-up by lifting the kettlebell up towards the ceiling. As you begin this movement, press both legs into the ground and squeeze your inner thighs together. This will help to stabilize your lower back.

Sit-Up, Ending Position

Sit up as straight as you can (which will depend on the flexibility of your shoulders, hamstrings and lower back). Even as you reach the seated posture, your legs should continue to be involved in stabilizing your entire body. Keep your neck long and shoulders down. As you sit-up, look up and in front of you. Imagine your spine lengthening and growing taller as you sit up. Avoid rounding forward.

Sit-Up, Ending Position with Leg Lift (added challenge)

The addition of a single leg lift is an added challenge. This is an option that should be attempted once you can complete a full set of the basic sit-ups. Lift one leg up as you approach the top of your sit-up. Keep the leg as straight as you can. You can perform the leg lift with the leg bent and bring the knee up as you sit-up. In either case, avoid rounding forward. Slowly return to the floor. If you choose this exercise, alternate legs on each repetition.

Turkish Get-up, Starting Position

This exercise is perfect for any style of martial art that does ground training. I stylize my Turkish Get-ups to mimic the basic ground get-up from the combat sports.

Begin by lying on your back with your left knee bent and left foot firmly placed on the ground. This means your right leg will be flat on the ground. You can start with the kettlebell lowered on the left side of your body, prepared to press straight up before the next phase of movement. Or, you can begin with the kettlebell raised in your left arm in a straight line above your shoulder while securely holding the kettlebell in your hand (this is harder). When learning this exercise it is ideal to begin with a light weight. I believe it is easier to learn with a weight in your hand (even if it is 2 pounds) than empty handed.

Turkish Get-up, Side Position (2)

Roll onto the right side of your body. Begin sitting upright while sliding your right arm along with the movement, so that you would end up being propped onto your right elbow. Engage the muscles in the side of your torso. As you do this side sit-up, the kettlebell must remain completely above your upper chest/shoulder. It is easiest to look up at the kettlebell when making this movement. This full transition from the lying position is fluid.

Turkish Get-Up, Base Position (3)

Slide your basing arm up close to your body. It should be underneath your shoulder. Your weight will shift onto the right side of your body. The kettlebell should continue to remain directly above your shoulder. This is fluid and moves dynamically into the next position.

Turkish Get-up, Base to Hip Press (4)

Drive your hips up, while controlling the kettlebell. Use the energy from combining all of these actions to generate the momentum you will need for the next phase of the exercise. During this phase, press the floor away as you lift your hips up. You will quickly move into the next position.

Turkish Get-up, Kneeling Post (5)

Continue to press the palm into the ground and engage you upper back muscles to continue moving to a standing position. Move the extended leg back and through the opening under your shoulder. As it passes under your body, place the knee on the ground. It is placed at a 90-degree angle. Keep lifting the kettlebell up over your shoulders and maintain good posture. This posture is your transition to getting up.

Turkish Get-up, Transition to Explosive Stand-up (6)

You will be getting up from this low lunge position. You should have a right angle at both knees. Connect the balls of the right foot (rear leg) to the ground to create an explosive get-up. The kettlebell continues to remain in a controlled overhead hold.

Turkish Get-up, Ending Position (7)

Stand up explosively! Utilize the muscles in both legs to lengthen your body up towards the ceiling. Use the free arm to assist with balance. As you stand, press the kettlebell up to the ceiling and look forward. Stay in control of the kettlebell at all times.

In order to return to the ground, reverse your positions. Make sure you are always controlling the kettlebell. If you find that this entire movement is difficult for your shoulder joint, lower the kettlebell down in the standing position and then re-press it to reverse the movements back into the starting position.

WEIGHT MACHINES

Chest Press

Whether you are using a conventional chest press machine or an incline chest press machine, it is important to first adjust your seat. The hand-bars of the machine should line up with the center of your chest (or the nipple line). Relax your shoulders and neck when positioning your hands on the handles. Once you are comfortable and have adjusted the weight, press the bar away from your chest without changing the position of your shoulders or creating an arch in your lower back. Always control the weight as you return it to the starting position.

Hamstring Curls

There are several different types of hamstring curl machines. This flatbed curl machine requires you to first adjust the cushions and position of the arm. Make sure the arm is close enough for you to comfortably curl your legs around it. Comfortably lie on the bed without arching your lower back. As you curl the weight, keep your hips pressing into the pads and your back in a neutral position. If you are using a different style machine, please read the instructions on the machine to make the proper adjustments.

Leg Extensions

There are a few adjustments to look for on the leg extension machine. First, make sure the seat is at the correct distance for you to be able to comfortably bend your knees. Then adjust the angle of the arm. If you have knee problems, you should create an angle closer to 90 degrees. A sharper, more acute, angle at the knees is more challenging. The third adjustment is the length of the pad on the arm that lies on top of your ankles. You may need to lengthen or shorten this piece of equipment. It should sit on your lower shin.

Once you have made the correct adjustments, you will sit straight up in the seat with your hips placed up against the back seat. As you extend the arm to straighten your legs, it is not necessary to lock your knees. As the weight returns, gently lower the arm. Each repetition should be slow and controlled.

Lat Pull Down

Most cable machines offer the wide bar attachment needed for this exercise. Once you have chosen your weight, grip the bar and sit. The width of your grip should be wider than your shoulders. As you pull the bar down towards your chest engage your abs and comfortably look up the cable. The bar should be pulled onto the upper section of chest about 3-6 inches below your chin. Avoid straining your neck when pulling the bar down. Every time you pull the bar, squeeze your shoulder blades together. As you release the bar, continue to keep your shoulder blades engaged.

Face Pulls

The face pull is best performed from a standing position. Attach the short bar on the bottom cable position. Begin with your knees slightly bent, shoulders back and neck long. Row the bar up towards your chin. As the bar approaches your upper chest squeeze your shoulder blades together. The elbows will bend and remain slightly above the shoulders. Avoid bending forward when you return the bar to the low cable.

Leg Press

This is technically a plate-loaded leg press. It is different than a leg press that requires the pin to be moved on the weight stack. Make sure you have made adjustments so you can comfortably sit in the machine. Most machines offer an extra small pad that can be placed behind your lower back if you need additional support.

Before un-racking the weight to lower it, place your feet about hip-width apart. As you press the weight up, you should be pressing through the center of your foot heels, not your toes. When the leg press sled lowers towards your body, make sure your knees stay in alignment with your toes. Ideally your knees will not bend past the front of your toes. Press your abs and the full length of your back against the seat during all phases of this exercise. If your gym has a different style leg press machine, read the instruction panel before beginning the exercise.

Squats

There are numerous styles of squat machines. This standing squat machine is similar to a squat rack. Like all machines, make sure you have adjusted the rack for your body before loading the weight. Comfortably place the shoulder pads on your shoulders and firmly grip the handles. Your feet should be placed in a comfortable width. As you bend your knees and sit back into the squat, keep the knees in line with your toes. Look up as you squat and keep your abs engaged. If your gym has a different style leg press machine, read the instruction panel before beginning the exercise.

PART IV

PROGRAM DESIGN

INTRODUCTION

P rogram design can be a fun challenge. In fact, it is the most creative aspect of fitness. I relate creating new training programs to a chef creating new recipes. In this case, the ingredients are all healthy, and the goal is to make as many healthy meals as possible. Even if you use the same 15-20 ingredients every week, you should be able to come up with a variety of healthy dishes.

When reflecting back on the exercises throughout this book, you will find many different types of programs. Each one has been written to provide a workout that places various demands on the body and accomplishes numerous training affects. These programs also make assumptions about your position on the athletic continuum. As you read through all the options listed, feel free to follow them in their entirety or break them down into pieces and mix and match. In general, it is best to begin with programs that look fun and immediately motivate you to workout.

DESIGNING A PROGRAM IS MASTERING CHANGE

We all utilize the words routine, program and workout interchangeably to refer to all types of training programs. But the goal is to create a training program that is hardly routine and one that provides you with more than just a good workout. The following sections will give you the tools to create strength training programs that enhance your martial arts skills, improve all areas of fitness and lengthen your practice.

Purposeful and structured change is the key to effective program design. You will soon read that change is the underlying theme of the principles of training. Muscular tissue is the most adaptable tissue in the body, and therefore, it responds to new training demands. The constant element of structured change will result in an increase in muscle size, strength, power and performance. As each principle of training is revealed, it will become clear how to manipulate the most tangible four variables—frequency, intensity, type, and time (FITT). Specifically, these are the frequency an exercise is performed, the intensity of the exercise, the type of exercise, and the amount of time before the exercises are complete. The way in which you choose to change these variables will culminate into your program.

Each structured change that is created will lead to a new phase of training. This structured change is the application of periodization, which will be described in detail below. You will come to understand that it is the most successful way to strength train for both muscular and cardiovascular improvements. Each program you create or choose from this book should be done for a specific period of time. Once you know the amount of time each program is going to last, you can begin to select the exercises that will be grouped together culminating into a strength program.

RECAPPING STRENGTH TRAINING

Let us summarize the details presented throughout this book. This will influence the exercises that you choose and how they could be organized:

- Gaining strength and improving function are not mutually exclusive goals. To enhance your absolute strength (one rep max) and functional strength your weight-training program must address more than just the muscles. Although our 360 joints are like hinges throughout the body that facilitate movement, they are not held together by simple hardware. The connective tissue, primarily the ligaments, supports the joints' range of movement in all directions. Therefore, all strength programs must involve exercises that strengthen the joints and connective tissue. This effort has a trickle-down effect of improving joint stability and mobility that does "pay forward" a contribution to helping build total body strength.

- Joint stability and mobility exercises contribute to the overall muscle dexterity when practicing your martial arts. The effort to add exercises that challenge your balance and joint health will improve your overall martial arts skills. It will also contribute to improving your power, the muscle's output of force and the muscle's strength.

- Dynamic flexibility exercises in your warm up and periodically throughout your workout will provide your body with a more fluent application of the muscles and joints for martial arts. Although static flexibility has always been a part of the traditional martial arts practice, it is best performed once the body is completely warmed up and the core body temperature has been raised (indicated by sweat, redness in your cheeks or elevated heart rate). Static flexibility does not have as direct an impact on functional movement or power. However, all forms of flexibility can prevent injuries and increase overall mobility, which will have a positive effect on improving your strength.

5 Questions to help you measure your weakness?

1. Do you have chronic pain anywhere?
2. Do you have extreme differences between your right and left side in strength or range of motion?
3. Do you have a joint that seems to be easily injured (i.e. an ankle)?
4. When you sit for a longer period of time and then get up, is any area 'locked up' or uncomfortably stiff?
5. Are you aware of a specific athletic weakness (i.e. coordination, balance, speed)?

DOES A FITNESS PROFESSIONAL NEED TO DESIGN YOUR STRENGTH TRAINING PROGRAM?

Many fitness professionals refer to program design as a science in itself. Although this is true in many cases, it is not necessary for it to become a daunting process. I compare exercise program design to cooking because anyone can learn to cook without formal training. It simply requires a set of principles and then a recipe to create a dish. The principles of cooking are simple: prepare food on a sanitized surface, use the right tools, combine ingredients at the correct time, use the proper temperature, clean up when you are done and then enjoy what you have made. Designing a strength training program is no different.

Fitness professionals and coaches use a set of principles to design strength training programs. Below are six principles of training: overload, progression, adaptation, specificity, recovery and reversibility. They should always be individually applied and you should always consider your position on the athletic continuum mentioned in the Getting Started section. As you read through them, be mindful of your strengths and weaknesses. Once you have a basic understanding how they are interrelated, you will be prepared to interpret all the programs included in this book and ultimately design your own strength training program.

Principles of Training Lead to Program Design

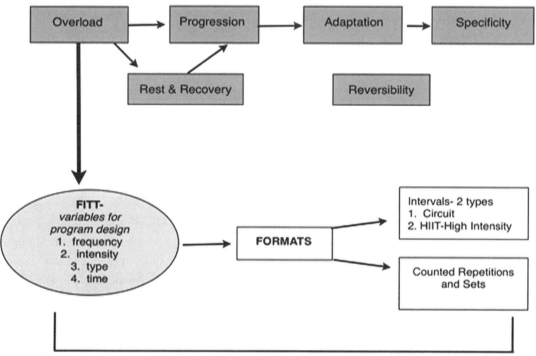

Structuring your chosen Frequency, Intensity, Type & Time (FITT) & the Format You will follow.

Periodization Methods

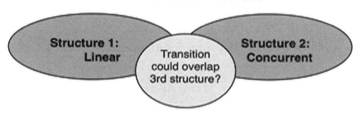

PHASES TO ORGANIZE
Total Body Strength/Flexible Mobility & Core
Hypertrophy/Flexible Mobility & Core
Absolute Strength = One-Rep-Max Strength/ Flexible Mobility & Core
Power/Flexible Mobility & Core
Muscular Endurance/Flexible Mobility & Core

THE PRINCIPLES OF TRAINING

Overload Principle

> *"The Overload Principle refers to improving muscular and cardiovascular strength and endurance by placing a higher demand than normal on the body or muscles, which ultimately improve performance and hopefully skill."*

Overload is the most acknowledged principle of training by the novice exerciser who hopes for increases in strength. Although it is commonly used, it is not always properly applied in a strength training program. The overload principle states that unless the body (muscles) is exposed to increased demands, it will not make improvements. This principle is actually true for muscular and cardiovascular strength. The overload principle overlaps with the principle of adaptation and progression. In order to achieve desired adaptations in your body, you must overload or stress it to stimulate the changes you seek. This principle applies to all areas of fitness. If you want to improve your muscular endurance for throwing more punches, you must expose the body to a demand for a longer period of time than was used in previous training sessions.

To make sure you follow big picture thinking about the overload principle, let us take it a couple steps further. Once the body adapts to the overload or stress, a stage of enhancement (i.e. strength, growth or both) occurs. Therefore, it is time again to progress and apply another increase in load or stress on the body to reach a new set of goals. Creating new goals is valuable, but our bodies do not experience an endless process of strength gains. What I find most fitness sources fail to mention is that the amount of true strength gains a person experiences is affected directly by many individual factors that can be considered uncontrollable. This includes some combination of age, injuries, starting point, muscular imbalances, hormone levels, origins of muscle insertions (clinical assessment) and genetics.

However, some controllable variables like diet, rest and hydration can contribute to off-setting some of the uncontrollable factors that limit progression. There will come a point even in a perfectly designed strength training program when you will no longer be able to simply increase the loads placed on the body. However, you can always create a variance in the training dynamic that offers a new stress that ultimately continues to improve your fitness, health, lean body mass and martial arts skills.

Most exercise science sources use the words demands, loads and stresses interchangeably. Although they have a similar meaning, I want to use demands as the general term and differentiate between load and stress. Technically, a load is a type of stress, but refers only to a metric, like weight. A stress can be a load, a training environment, an outside stimulus and many other external variables. I am going to present a tailored and broader definition of the overload principle for the martial artist. It applies to improving muscular and cardiovascular strength and endurance by placing a higher demand than normal on the body or muscles, which ultimately improve performance and hopefully skill.

There are guidelines that help you properly apply this principle. The laws of overload are implemented by learning how to use –FITT—frequency, intensity, type and time.

The FITT variables are relevant in each training principle. You can create a strength training program with the FITT variables that is customized for any level of fitness and for any set of goals. Each one of these variables has a direct impact on overload, progression, adaptation and improvement of specific sport skills. Frequency of an exercise, its intensity, the type of exercise and the time it is performed can be adjusted in numerous ways to create dynamic, innovative and motivating workout programs.

Progression Principle

"Although many progressions are simple increases in weight or repetitions, you cannot expect them to occur equally from one muscle to another, or one exercise to another."

Progression must be appropriate in all training programs. It must consider your position on the athletic continuum and acknowledge your weaknesses or limitations. The principle of progression shares its roots with adaption, overload and specificity of the martial art (defined directly below). Progression is not an evenly applied change. It is not a blanket change or one that occurs across the board. Additionally, progressions are not always metric in nature; they can be the introduction of a new dynamic, like instability (i.e. taking a bicep curl from the ground to a balance platform) to an exercise. Although many progressions are simple increases in weight or repetitions, you cannot expect them to occur equally from one muscle to another, or one exercise to another. It is important to consider this fact when drafting your training goals and expectations. Whichever way you choose to increase a demand on the body to stimulate a new adaptation will lead to some level of progression.

Adaptation Principle

"As you continue to create purposeful progressions in your training program, your body will adapt and you will then introduce new ones."

Every time you introduce a new training stress in your workout, your body responds. The response may be improved reaction time, increased strength or more power. This response is called adaptation. Adaptation combined with recovery elevates athletic skills and performance. As you continue to create purposeful progressions in your training program, your body will adapt and you will then introduce new ones. As with progressions, the muscles and systems of the body do not follow the same time schedule for every adaptation that is achieved. Be mindful of this fact so you can adjust your expectations and use it as a way to assess if the changes you are making in your program are the correct ones.

Specificity Principle

> *"This principle prioritizes the most applicable exercises*
> *to your specific martial art."*

Specificity is one of the most relevant themes to address in all strength training programs for a martial artist. This principle prioritizes the most applicable exercises that specifically enhance sport movements and the overall demands of the sport. It does not set aside the value of developing general strength or the need to practice your specific martial art. In our case as martial artists, it is punching, kicking, stances, throwing and landing. I must point out however, we continue to characterize martial arts by these techniques, but there is a huge variance from one style to another. In order for you to comprehensively benefit from the information presented throughout this book, you must keep reminding yourself of the specific movements most relevant in your style. Create a top ten list that prioritizes your martial arts sports skills, and make sure your strength training does not lose sight of them as you pick and choose different training exercises and modalities.

Recovery Principle

> *"To achieve any gain in strength from a workout,*
> *you must provide the body with an appropriate amount of rest."*

Progressions and adaptations are not instantaneous. In order to achieve any gain in strength from a workout, you must provide the body with an appropriate amount of rest. The rest allows the muscle tissue to recover. Let us jump back to the overload principle. When you place a demand on the muscle, like a heavier load, it causes mini-traumas to the actual muscle fibers and connective tissues. When they are at a state of rest, they repair themselves. This process of repair actually rebuilds and strengthens the tissue involved. This is true for all fitness systems, such as muscular strength, power, endurance and cardiovascular performance.

Rest and recovery is also valuable during training sets and in-between workout sessions. The amount of rest between sets and exercises will depend on how your exercise is bracketed. For example, a weight that is challenging at the 4th, 5th and 6th (for a 6 rep set) rep will require a long period of rest, perhaps 2-4 minutes before another set can be performed of the same exercise. However, an exercise that does not cause fatigue until the 13th rep may be able to be repeated after 30-45 seconds of a break.

Although the aforementioned examples give you a definite time with relation to the type of weight lifting bracket, there are some factors that will influence rest and recovery every time you train. Some of the most common factors that influence the amount of rest and recovery required post-workout includes intensity, age, diet, sleep and overall health. High intensity exercise will have a profound impact on how long it will take for your body to recover. Age impacts the amount of recovery needed before adaptation can occur because of the nervous system. But also be aware of your current baseline of fitness, the overall status of your health (i.e. did you just recover from a cold), and your martial arts training schedule.

Reversibility Principle

*"If the stress is removed or decreased,
there will be a decrease in that particular area of muscular,
or cardiovascular strength, or endurance."*

The concept of reversibility could be eliminated from the training principles and can simply become a governing fact. It refers to regression. If the stress is removed or decreased, there will be a decrease in that particular area of muscular, or cardiovascular strength, or endurance. Regression does occur when the training demands are no longer placed on the body. We have all experienced this after a long break from the martial arts or from a workout. Whether it is due to illness or a vacation, the body can lose strength, endurance, power, flexibility and cardiovascular capabilities. Just as none of these fitness systems progress and adapt at the same rate, they also do not regress equally.

Do not fret if you decide to take a break from training. Muscle memory can be relied upon to regain a portion of the strength and skill you once had. But this only applies to those that had it to begin with. For example, if you are beginning a training program in your 40s that includes strengthening your legs, it may be hard to know exactly when you have reached your peak. Unless you have something to compare it to from your younger years, reversibility may not have occurred. Of course we can all generally say, "I was so much stronger when I was younger."

On the other hand, if you played football in college and you have not actively been strength training for a decade, then regression has occurred. However, you can rebuild that strength with a proper strength-training program in your 30s or 40s.

HOW SHOULD I FORMAT MY PROGRAM?

The principles of overload, progression, adaptation, specificity, recovery and reversibility offer an explanation of why it is not effective to follow the same strength and conditioning program. When the overload principle is applied properly, it ignites a proper sequencing for improvement to take place in all areas of fitness. Changing FITT of your exercises helps to keep your strength training workouts fun and motivating. There are two basic formats that you can use to help organize the way in which your exercises will be done—intervals, and counted repetitions and sets. Recognizing when and how to manipulate the FITT variables are simple once you have chosen the format you would like to use.

FORMAT TYPE 1: INTERVALS

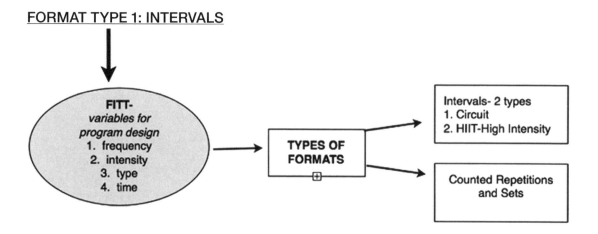

An interval format refers to the period of time the muscle is under tension. The muscles do not actually count repetitions, but it knows how long it has been under a specific amount of tension. Tension can be placed on a muscle for 10, 20, 30 or 60-second intervals of time. Regardless of the amount of time you choose, you should be experiencing a high level of intensity towards the last 20% of the interval. You can also develop strength, muscular endurance, mobility, balance, martial arts skills and power during an interval training program. Interval training can be organized into two basic formats. Although there are many popular interval classes offered at most local health clubs like Boot Camp, Tabata Training (8 rounds of 20 second intervals with 10 seconds of rest that = 4 minutes), Pyramids (10 sec, 20 sec, 30 sec, 30 sec, 20 sec, 10 sec) and Progressives (1 rep, 2 reps, 3 reps, 4 reps, etc .. up to 10), they are all versions of the two styles described below.

STYLES OF INTERVALS

Circuit training is often thought of a series of exercise stations that work the body in various ways. The exercises can be organized by many different categories (i.e. power exercises), muscle groups (i.e. legs and arms), equipment (i.e. medicine ball and kettlebell) or represent a little of everything (i.e. dumbbells, kettlebell, plyometric, cable machine, etc...). Most circuit interval workouts that focus on muscular strength include 4 to 8 stations in one series, with 2-4 sets of each exercise. Keep in mind, that circuit training formats offer the most versatility and creative opportunities. It is the easiest and most adaptable program design. It also works in all types of workout settings and with limited equipment.

High intensity interval training (HIIT) or threshold training is another form of interval training. It is a highly specialized format that uses short, high-intensity exercises and movements to increase the heart rate above 80% of the target heart rate. Often the intensity will remain almost the same throughout this type of interval program. Therefore, the exercise type, frequency and time are changed from one HIIT program to another.

This type of HIIT is often referred to as threshold training because the exercises chosen are done at an intensity that will push you to your threshold (best measured by perceived rate of exertion). This level of intensity makes it difficult to even say a few words and most give it an RPE score of 9 or 10 (see chart below). Because this type of training increases the heart rate significantly, it is not recommended for the new exerciser or someone with a poor ability to assess their level of exertion. Although HIIT is being listed as a separate category of interval training, it can be performed in a circuit style as well. Many of the sub-categories presented in this section can be combined.

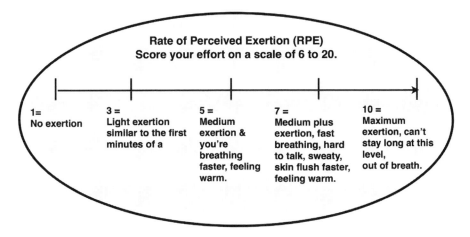

HIIT or threshold training is one of the most innovative and progressive training styles in athletics today. It increases the amount of calories burned both during and post-workout. It not only boosts your metabolism, improves power, but also enhances cardiovascular and anaerobic output. HIIT workouts can be done with a wide variety of strength exercises from bodyweight exercises to kettlebells, medicine balls to dumbbells, and tires to sandbags. When strength exercises are assigned to a HIIT format, the exercises must be technically performed and the exerciser must not compromise the form of the movement (another reason why it is not an ideal format for a novice exerciser).

Muscular Fatigue verse Muscular Failure

HIIT is a physically demanding format. Therefore, you must be able to differentiate between muscle fatigue and failure. Fatigue occurs when you feel a burning sensation, yet still have the ability to control the movement. Failure is when you feel as though you might collapse or lose control of your body or equipment. I recommend experimenting with HIIT as some point in your training. It is a highly successful format for improving overall athletic performance. If you decide to use high intensity interval training, remember that the intensity should not surpass the technique of the movement or exercise. To maximize the benefits, you must always apply the principles of rest and recovery.

FORMAT TYPE 2: COUNTED REPETITIONS AND SETS

The most conventional style of programming is counted reps and sets. The numbers of repetitions you perform are grouped into a set. A set refers to the point at which you begin an exercise that is performed consecutively until you stop and rest, or move onto another type of exercise. When you make a decision to perform a set of 8, 10 or 12 reps, it is called bracketing your reps and sets. There is a logical correlation between the difficulty of the weight you are lifting and the bracketing it follows. For example, if you are lifting a weight for only 4 to 6 reps, it is assumed the weight is at least 70% of your maximum lifting capacity. It also implies you are working very hard by the 3rd rep in that set. This type of bracketing is considered to have the goal of absolute strength gains. A set that includes 10 reps implies the weight you are lifting is challenging by the 6th or 7th rep, and therefore, focused on general strength gains and hypertrophy (increase in muscle size). A set that includes 12 to 20 repetitions is associated with goals of muscular endurance. The bracket you choose must reflect your goals.

Intervals can also be quantified (i.e. number of reps and timed interval) by counting and tracking the number of repetitions completed in each interval of time. However, most studies in the exercise sciences defer to counted reps and sets that are bracketed to quantify strength improvements. In fact, counted reps and sets is a great tool for the novice exerciser. It will reveal clear improvements in muscular strength and even muscular endurance.

The Big Picture - Structuring Your Programs Over the Course of a Year

Periodization refers to simply dividing your overall training program into specific phases. It is the most strategic method of organizing your strength training program. Although periodization can be applied in varying degrees, it is important even if you are a novice at strength training to create some changes in your program approximately every 4 weeks. You can use either format of training (intervals or counted reps and sets), but structured change must occur in order to maximize your strength training efforts.

I will provide you with two separate categories of periodization: linear and concurrent. They have their own definitions, but can overlap at some point in a strength training program. Below is a description of each training structure along with their drawbacks and benefits. Consider several factors when choosing which is most suitable for your martial arts strength and conditioning program. First, prioritize your athletic needs. Remember you are trying to improve your performance and practice of your martial art or combat sport. For example, if you have always been a fairly strong person, but your reaction time is slow, then speed and power training should become a focus. Your personal goals will influence how you arrange the FITT variables. Continuously reflect on your position on the athletic continuum.

Second, there is no single "best" way to structure strength training programs for all martial artists. The differences in body types, gender, genetics, body composition, injuries, health, fitness levels and age will constantly impact the way you apply periodization. Even if you adapt the concepts in this book, use the programs already created or design your own from scratch. You may change your style of periodization after 3, 6 or 12 months.

By periodizing your program, you are simply committing to 3 fundamental things:

1.) You will make changes in your strength and conditioning program every 3 to 6 weeks.
2.) You are anticipating adaptations and need to forecast the progressions you will make over a long period of time, not just for that short phase.
3.) You have the big picture in mind. You have short-term goals that help you move closer to your long-term goals, which will actually improve your martial arts skills and overall fitness permanently. This way of approaching your programming will efficiently manage your weaknesses and limitations.

TYPES OF PERIODIZATION

Linear Periodization

There are two basic forms of periodization. The conventional format focuses on one set of goals at a time. It is called linear periodization. Most organize their linear phases in the following order: muscular endurance, hypertrophy, strength, power and then a form of transition or restoration. The progression usually begins with a higher number of reps that are low intensity (i.e. brackets of 10-15 reps) and progresses to phases that perform a low number of repetitions at high intensity (i.e. brackets of 4, 5, 6, reps).

Benefits

Linear periodization is an attractive structure for some because it is simple to follow. It is also ideal for some specialized athletes (i.e. power lifters). As you go through the various phases over and over which become cycles, you will improve all fitness systems to some degree in the very end (an undetermined amount of time). This can be comforting for a beginner or young adult who simply wants to gain strength and size. Furthermore, a linear structure has a certain amount of predictability and offers quantitative proof of your strength improvements.

Drawbacks

The criticism of this type of periodization is that while it develops one goal, it is at the expense of another goal. So while you are focused on building strength and lifting heavy weights at lower reps, you are losing the muscular endurance that is also relevant for sport performance.

Concurrent Periodization

The type of periodization that I prefer for most martial artists is called concurrent periodization. A concurrent structure essentially trains several goals during one short phase, but often with a slightly greater emphasis on one goal. After reading how concurrent is defined, you can recognize that it offers a lot of organizational freedom. There are many categories of concurrent periodization. I recommend creating a sequence for the various workouts that schedule muscular endurance, cardiovascular conditioning, strength, hypertrophy and power without compromising your martial arts training.

Concurrent periodization does not train all goals in the same workout. They are generally dispersed over a 1-week period of time. I prefer the concurrent model, but I suggest dispersing the various goals over a 14 to 21 day period of time. I believe this allows for sufficient time at your martial arts school training your required techniques and skills, while still allowing time for recovery. During one cycle, you can focus more attention on a specific goal like power. You would, therefore, choose more exercises, which develop overall power for martial arts, and some that are sport specific. Then, after 14-21 days, begin a new phase with a new focus. A new phase can focus on total body strength gains, but continue to train a handful of power exercises.

Benefits

It is not uncommon that a traditional martial artist would train a combination of skills within in a one-week period of time. This can include forms, sparring, traditional components, punching and kicking. Within one week of classes, your training will need endurance, speed, strength, balance, flexibility and power. Concurrent periodization can successfully include workouts for each of these fitness systems, without losing the progress you have made in a specific area.

Concurrent periodization supports the need for a lifestyle that is also ever changing. To remind you of Bruce Lee's reference of an old Chinese proverb, "The wise adapt themselves to circumstances, as water moulds itself to the pitcher." I mention this because being able to constantly adapt your strength and conditioning program to coincide with your martial arts training without compromising any goal, will also lengthen your martial arts practice.

Drawbacks

One could argue that concurrent periodization is complicated and requires a multi-tasker's mindset. I agree with this criticism since there are so many moving pieces to keep track of over the 14-21 day period of time. For a novice exerciser, it may seem overwhelming. When scheduling the various training goals over a one-cycle period, sufficient rest and recovery must be assigned in-between workouts that are high intensity. Therefore, some argue that a concurrent style of training develops more injuries due to overuse and insufficient recovery. You can refer to the schedules listed below for examples of concurrent training.

Athletes in the martial arts are different than athletes that play one specific position (i.e. a pitcher). Therefore, I encourage martial artists to leverage their heighten sense of awareness. Listen to your body. Improving all systems simultaneously can be successfully done for all different types of martial artists and combat sports practitioners.

Example of a Traditional Linear Periodization Program Over a 6 Month Period

January- 4 weeks	Muscular Endurance
February and March – 6-8 weeks	Hypertrophy
March through April – 6 -8 weeks	Absolute Strength
May through June – 6 – 8 weeks	Power

Example of Traditional Concurrent Periodization Program over 1-week
(each / is equal to one day)

Each Week: Strength/Hypertrophy/ Rest / Muscular Endurance/ Power/ Rest/ Rest

Example of a Concurrent Periodization Program over 2 weeks
(each / is equal to one day)

Week 1: Muscular Endurance/ Power/ Rest/ Hypertrophy/ Strength Upper Body/ Rest/ Strength

Week 2: Lower Body/ Rest / Power/ Hypertrophy/ Rest/ Strength Total Body/ Hypertrophy

Example of a Concurrent Periodization Program over a 3-week program
(each / is equal to one day)

Week 1: Muscular Endurance/ Hypertrophy/Power/ Rest/ Strength Upper Body/ Rest/ Strength

Week 2: Lower Body/ Rest / Muscular Endurance/ Power/ Rest/ Strength Total Body/ Hypertrophy

How much rest do you need in a concurrent program?	How much rest do you need in a linear program?
1 week phase = 2 days 2 week phase = 4 days	Absolute Strength- 48 hour minimum Hypertrophy - 24 hour minimum

AGE MATTERS, DO NOT FOOL YOURSELF

If we had to divide our athletic development phases into three categories (for simplicity purposes), it would be as follows:

- Adolescences – until 21 years old
- Adulthood – 21 to 35 years old
- Mature Adulthood – 35 to 55 years of age

There are exceptions to these categories; a fourth could be added at any age for women who experience motherhood or anyone that suffers a severe injury requiring extensive rehabilitation. This additional developmental phase would focus on recovery and reestablishing a fitness baseline, while regaining overall functionality.

Age should influence the structure, intensity and exercises you chose for strength and conditioning. If you are beginning a structured strength and conditioning program to enhance your martial arts skills after the age of 35, I discourage one-rep-max programs. Even a well-designed phase of absolute strength comes with its drawbacks. As weights increase only allowing for 3, 4 and 5 reps, the joints become highly stressed. It may result in some strength gains, but at the expense of having healthy joints and connective tissue. Furthermore, it is not likely to translate into heightened martial arts performance. Therefore, I do not recommend it for the average mature adult.

Total Body Strength (TBS) is a more suitable goal. Moreover, strength and speed must work in harmony to translate into power, which will improve your martial arts skills. Another modality of strength training that offers tremendous value is body weight exercises (see *Bodyweight Training for the Martial Athlete* in Part I). There are many ways to intensify bodyweight training that is mindful of preserving joint health. You can choose to insert these modalities of strength training in a linear or concurrent structure. Both structures require proper recovery regardless of the structure. Recovery for adults over 35 is significantly slower than those in their 20s. This statement holds true for every 5-year increment over the age of 40 years old. An absolute training phase is not necessary for developing and maintaining strength for martial artists between the ages 35 to 55 years of age, verse younger practitioners between 21 to 35 years old.

If you have spent time between the ages of 21 and 35 developing strength, it is fairly easy to maintain that strength after the age of 35. Most athletes achieve enormous strength gains during the ages of 21 to 35 because the years prior to this period have been spent dedicated to playing sports or skill driven activities. This leaves the decade between 20 and 30 with ample opportunity to build strength. Therefore, traditional one-rep-max workouts (or phases) that are usually dedicated to improving absolute strength during these prime years offer a valuable training experience without jeopardizing joint health. Most of the exercises included in traditional one-rep-max workouts (using maximum loads at low reps) include versions of the bench press, leg press, deadlift, squat, clean and snatch, lat pull down, face pull, bicep curl, triceps press down and shoulder press. Although these exercises can be continued at any age, it is the intensity of the weight and bracket of repetitions that should be carefully considered. Absolute strength training regiments may jeopardize the opportunity for you to experience a 'pain-free' training program that enhances your martial arts.

Over 35 Years Old, Let us Review

One-rep-max workouts do not translate directly into heightening martial arts skills because they pose some drawbacks that stem from the natural changes that occur in the body due to age. Getting older does pose a wide array of degenerative issues. But on an optimistic note, the exercise science and nutrition data available over the past decade has demonstrated that we may not be able to prevent some factors associated with age, but they can be slowed down with a good diet and proper exercise. Here are some factors that impact the length of rest required and the need for longer and more thorough warm-ups when training over the age of 35, 40, 50, and so on:

- Human Growth Hormone and Testosterone levels peak in the late teens to early 20s. This time is optimal for strength gains and muscular growth. These levels are significantly lower over the age of 35.
- The toll of being active over more years creates more vulnerability and may lead to more injuries when workouts do not include an appropriate intensity to rest ratio.
- As you get older, synovial fluid production (the liquid in the joints) decreases because of hormonal changes. Because of this, the body requires more time warming up.
- Your base strength has been elevated over years of training. This base-line of strength is one you have earned. The muscles will remember movement (muscle memory) it has previously learned and the body can regain a good portion of strength once developed.
- With years of active living, strength training and martial arts practice, comes the need to properly care for the joints to prevent or manage joint related injuries.

DEFINING PHASES, CYCLES AND DAILY GOALS:

6 Safety Tips for Heavy Lifting

1. Use a spotter for free weights when:
- the bar crosses your face or head
- the bar is on your back
- the weight is racked across your chest

2. Spotting dumbbell exercises should:
- be done at the forearms
- place hands near the weights
- be done by someone that can lift the weight themselves

3. Communicate with the spotter
- about the lift difficulty
- if you have failed at the lift before
- a clear verbal signal for help

4. Use collars with all free weights/bars.

5. Make sure you bench and position is stable.

6. Don't hold your breath when you are lifting.

The following are various types of training cycles or goals. The brief explanations below represent the basic criteria for each of these phases/goals. These phases can be inserted into the structure of a linear or concurrent periodization model. Therefore, each one can be followed for a 3-6 week period as the sole focus, typical of the linear model. Or, they can all be layered within one training cycle over a 7-21 day period of time, found in various types of concurrent models. Although I believe that all of these phases offer the martial artist value, remember that you first need to consider your weaknesses or limitations and how they relate to your position on the athletic continuum. You will manipulate all or some of the phases in all the programs you create. The frequency of an exercise, the intensity of an exercise, the bracket of reps or time you are under tension will be under your control. The way you use the FITT variables reflects one of these phases below.

TBS – Total Body Strength (including Flexible Mobility and Core) can be bracketed in a couple different ways. The exercises and efforts made during this phase accomplish many important long-term goals. It is what I consider a 10-rep routine. The exercises you choose should offer a challenge at the 7-10th rep. It is most often done for a total of 3 sets, but sometimes 4. Although the overall goal is to build strength throughout the body, it is does not mean every workout focuses on each muscle group. You can do all muscle groups in one workout or divide it up into the pushing and pulling muscles.

If you decide to pair up muscle groups in a three-day program, I suggest the following pairings. Include balance exercises and dynamic flexibility into the warm-up and cool down for each program.

- Pulling Actions: Back, Biceps, Core, Body Weight (i.e. pull-ups), *ideally include some exercises with rotation.*
- Pushing Actions: Chest, Triceps, Shoulders, Core (i.e. push-ups) *ideally include some exercises with rotation* (including shoulder stability)
- Legs and Rotation: Squats, Lunges, Calves, Torso Rotation Exercises (i.e. core with twisting actions) *ideally includes flexibility training.*

If you are dividing the body up into two parts, I suggest the following. Include balance exercises and dynamic flexibility into the warm-up and cool down for each program.

- Pulling Actions and Legs: Back, Biceps, Lower Back, Shoulders (including shoulder stability), Legs (i.e. multi-joint movements like squats, leg press, lunges).
- Pushing Actions and Rotation: Chest, Shoulders, Triceps and Core with Rotations.

You could consider this phase the insurance phase. Most of the exercises performed at this time will help to ensure that the other phases are not stipend by injuries and poor mobility. The general strength you are gaining at this time will lay the foundation for future phases of training. It is helpful if you are also developing solid cardiovascular fitness and have the ability to incorporate balance training. The exercises in this phase should always focus on large muscle groups like legs, chest and back. Exercises for the arms, calves and core can be incorporated into the routines, but the goal is to always focus most of your efforts in multi-joint actions. If you decide to incorporate power lifting or advanced kettlebell training, your focus should first be on perfecting your technique. This will maximize your efforts in future phases or on training days that use these exercises.

Hypertrophy (with Flexible Mobility and Core) is simply the enlargement of the muscle. This is a gratifying phase because there is often an increase in lean body mass. A hypertrophy phase can be used to improve athletic performance, as well as increase the size the muscle cells. You will most likely do 3 to 5 sets and 8 to 12 reps, experiencing a challenge at the 6th rep. The time the muscle is under tension can also be manipulated by slowing down the speed of the exercise being performed.

The organization of muscle groups can follow the same pairings described in the TBS Phase. You can do all muscles in one routine if that is what your schedule permits, or you can break the body up into 2 or 3 parts.

Absolute Strength or One-Rep-Max (with Flexible Mobility and Core) can also be thought of as building your maximum strength. This phase mostly follows a counted rep and set format that is structured as follows: 3-6 sets of an exercise with 2-5 reps per set. This phase requires long periods of rest in-between each set. The stress of the load requires a careful warm up for each muscle group to avoid injuries and often the need of a spot (a person assisting you with your weight). Furthermore, because of the intensity, it is not suggested to do all muscle groups in one workout session. It is best to divide the body up into 2 or 3 groups (see chart).

Your efforts during this phase, cycle or training day will culminate into you lifting a heavier weight than you have lifted up until that day. With this being said, to maximize the benefits of this phase you are not obligated to move up in every exercise or for every muscle group.

Power (and Flexible Mobility and Core) is a fun phase. It is the combination of strength and speed. Power often manipulates the time component of the FITT variables in a clever way. Power training increases how much force you can produce in a specific movement.

Power training is difficult with conventional weight training exercises because of the way tempo is manipulated. Not every weight exercise can increase in speed without causing risk to the supporting joints and connective tissue. This risk comes from the need to decelerate the load with control before accelerating it once again. As discussed earlier, it is best to include ballistic and plyometric exercises as the majority of your program when focused on power. Ideal training tools for a power phase includes medicine balls, kettlebells, body weight, boxes and even sand bags.

Power training can be done using an interval or counted rep and set format. I personally enjoy timed intervals and experiment with brackets of 10 to 60 seconds. Otherwise, use 4-8 sets at 5-10 reps as a guide. Remember that the intensity should increase the shorter the set or interval. The goal is to improve reaction time and become quicker when executing your martial arts skills.

Muscular Endurance (with Flexible Mobility and Core) is an important phase of training. It is generally focused on the muscle's ability to work over a long period of time. Therefore, muscle mass is somewhat secondary. Training for muscular endurance requires sets 3-4 sets up to 20 repetitions. The rest interval between sets is usually short, about 30 seconds. In order to build endurance, there must be an underlying level of strength. Without a baseline of strength, the muscles would simply be too weak to perform any repetitive movement. Muscular endurance is clearly a valuable fitness system for martial arts. It will improve punching and kicking.

As a series of exercises challenges the muscles, the ability to sustain repeated contractions usually increases the heart rate. Therefore, many people also use muscular endurance programs as a way to assist with weight loss. One popular program format is circuit training. This type of format is ideal for building muscular endurance. Unlike muscular strength phases, total body workouts do not pose many problems, but you can also divide the body up into 2 or 3 sections.

A muscular endurance phase can follow a timed interval or counted rep and set format. I believe that one of the biggest values of this phase is that it offers a mental break from high intensity workouts. I have often defaulted to this phase and sometimes call it a maintenance workout. Maintenance training can be done when you are travelling, on vacation or need to take a break from using a joint or muscle due to an injury. Additionally, this phase allows for a focus to be placed on injury management, strengthening connective tissue and improving joint stability.

Summarizing Program Design

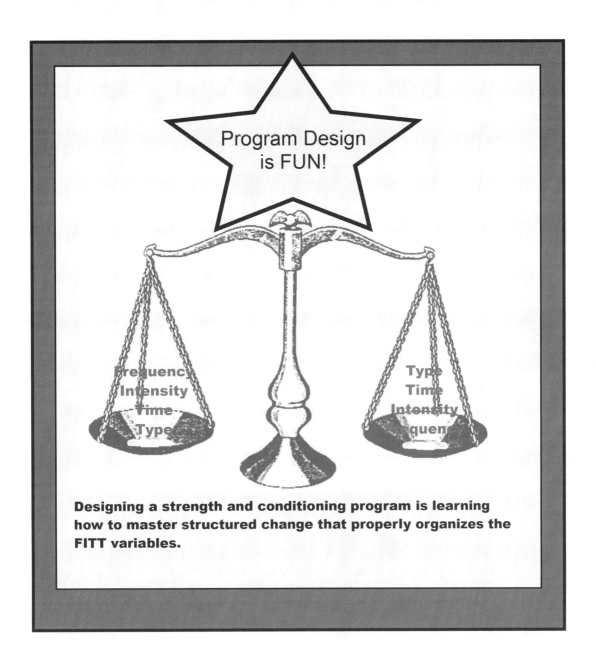

Designing a strength and conditioning program is learning how to master structured change that properly organizes the FITT variables.

There are 6 basic principles of training.
1. Overload - place a higher demand on the body to force it to adapt.
2. Progression - change the demand appropriately which progresses you from where you were originally or in your first training session.
3. Adaptation - the body will adapt to new demands placed on it; increasing strength, endurance and stability.
4. Specificity - prioritize the most important exercises for martial arts or injury management. Make sure they are represented in your program.
5. Rest - without proper rest and recovery time the adaptation principle will not work. The body needs to rest in-between the exercises and from workout to workout. Without rest and recovery, the body may be prone to injuries.
6. Reversibility - also refers to regression. If you stop training certain fitness systems, you will lose some of the improvements you have achieved. However, the body does not experience reversibility at the same rate, regression is relative.

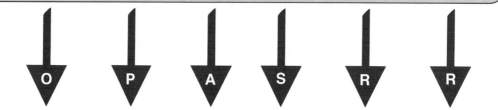

O   P   A   S   R   R

These principle help you organize your program over the course of a 1 month, 3 month, 6 month or 12 month period.

Intervals in a Circuit or High

FORMAT TYPES

Counted Reps & Sets

Use perceived rate of exertion to figure out if you can train harder. Listen to your body & heart if you can push yourself harder.

Ask Yourself?

1. How often do you want to make changes in your program?
2. Do you want to focus on developing one area of fitness at a time?
3. Or, do you want to work on a couple goals at once?

What do my answers mean?

1. The type of periodization that is right for me.
2. If I want one goal at a time, then a linear program is better for me.
3. If I prefer several goals at once, then a concurrent program is better for me.

What is linear periodization?

1. It develops one goal at a time.
2. You may lose enhancements made in one area while working on a new goal.
3. It is very easy to structure, usually follows a standard 4 week period.
4. There is a certain amount of predictability.

What is concurrent periodization?

1. Training several goals at once.
2. Must be careful to allow for proper recovery.
3. Very adaptable, works with a busy lifestyle.
4. Can be overwhelming to manage all goals in a 7, 14 or 21 day period.

What are my program goals?

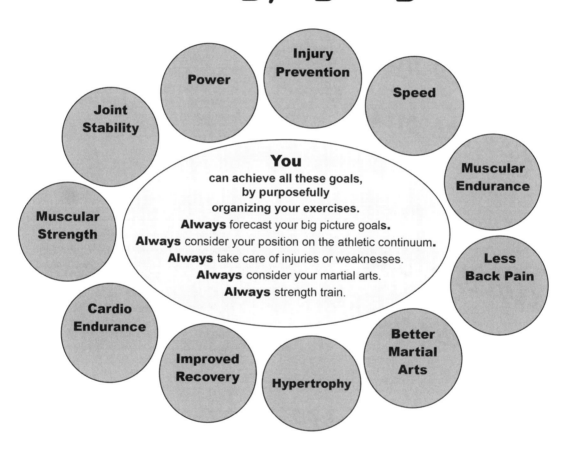

Power

Injury Prevention

Speed

Joint Stability

Muscular Endurance

Muscular Strength

Less Back Pain

You
can achieve all these goals,
by purposefully
organizing your exercises.
Always forecast your big picture goal**s**.
Always consider your position on the athletic continuum**.**
Always take care of injuries or weaknesses.
Always consider your martial arts.
Always strength train.

Cardio Endurance

Improved Recovery

Hypertrophy

Better Martial Arts

What factors influence the exercises that are best ?

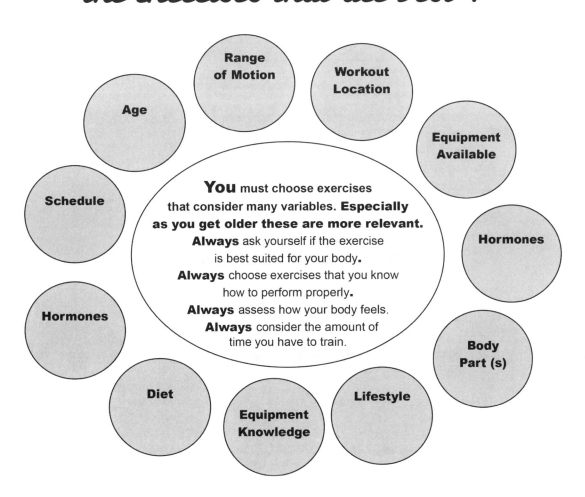

You must choose exercises that consider many variables. **Especially as you get older these are more relevant.** **Always** ask yourself if the exercise is best suited for your body. **Always** choose exercises that you know how to perform properly. **Always** assess how your body feels. **Always** consider the amount of time you have to train.

Range of Motion

Workout Location

Age

Equipment Available

Schedule

Hormones

Hormones

Body Part (s)

Diet

Equipment Knowledge

Lifestyle

How can I begin dividing my body up?

Two Day Programs

DAY ONE: Total Body including Sport Specific

DAY TWO: Total Body including Sport Specific

DAY ONE: Pulling Actions - Back, Biceps, Core, Body Weight, Joint Stability, Flexibility

DAY TWO: Pushing Actions & Legs - Chest, Triceps, Shoulders, Legs, Core with Rotation

Three Day Programs

DAY ONE: Pulling Actions - Back, Biceps, Core, Body Weight, Joint Stability, Flexibility

DAY TWO: Legs & Stability, Core

DAY THREE: Pushing Actions - Chest, Triceps, Shoulders, Legs, Core with Rotation

DAY ONE: Legs, Body Weight, Core with Rotation

DAY TWO: Pulling Actions - Back, Biceps, Core

DAY THREE: Pushing Actions - Chest, Triceps, Shoulders, Core with Rotation

PART V

PROGRAMS

The programs provided in this section are a representation of several different goals and types of cycles. These are sample programs. There are hundreds of other ways to combine the various exercises provided in this book. These sample programs are a great place to start. Make sure you read through the various icons and abbreviations to learn their meaning.

It is important to choose the most suitable workout program. The amount of time you have to train and your training environment will impact your options. Each program is this section has icons on the side of the page that will give you key information about the program. For example, do not choose a workout that is intended for a gym environment if you are training at home. Make sure you have the equipment available in order to complete the exercises listed. You will also find that every program is divided into rounds. I choose this style to highlight how every training program is actually comprised of many short-term goals. I have organized these goals into individual rounds. A round includes all the repetitions and sets for the exercises listed.

Before beginning any of these programs read the icons. The icons will give you the following information. The key for the icons and abbreviations is below. Read through them, since they are used consistently in all of the programs included in this book.

- the title and general goal of the program
- the ideal setting to complete the workout
- estimated length of time
- required skill level if any
- whether it is suitable for individuals with various injuries

Key for Icons and Abbreviations

HWT	=	Heavy Weights
MWT	=	Medium Weights
LWT	=	Light Weights
PLYO	=	Plyometric Training or Explosive Training
KB	=	Kettle Bell
DB	=	Dumbbell
r	=	Repetitions
SB	=	Straight Bar or Rack

PROGRAM ICONS

 Location

 Length of time

 Workout Level

 Not suggested if you are experiencing shoulder pain or recovering from a shoulder injury.

 Not suggested if you are experiencing back pain or recovering from a back injury.

 Not suggested if you are experiencing knee pain or recovering from a knee injury.

 This is an advanced program for a person who has good weight lifting form and has been strength training or working out regularly for 6 months.

 This exercise has a sport specific application for the martial arts.

 This is one of my favorite programs with many of my favorite exercises.

TOTAL BODY STRENGTH TRAINING

Round 1
- 12-20r decline push ups
- 10r arm circles each side, both directions
- 20r air squats
- Hamstring stretches
- 10r pelvic bridges

Round 2
- 6-8r chest press/ HWT
- 10r single leg squats with ground touches per leg
- 6-8r pull-ups, add band for assistance or weight for challenged
- Repeat x 4 increase weight for challenge

Round 3
- 6-8r leg press or split squat/ HWT
- 10r walking push ups moving side to side
- 6-8r lat pull down/HWT
- Repeat x 4 increase weight for challenge

Round 4
- 6-8r arnold press with DB /HWT
- 25r V-sits
- 6-8r plank row with DB/HWT
- Repeat x 4 increase weight for challenge

Round 5
- Alternating Leg lifts
- Stretches

Notes and Date

Gym Workout

40-50 minutes

Any Level

FAV

written by Katalin Ogren

TOTAL BODY CONDITIONING

Round 1
- 1 minute shadow boxing
- 10 arm circles in each direction
- 10 alternating lunges
- 30 seconds plank
- 10 push ups

Gym Workout

Round 2
- Plyo: 10r box jumps, then 30 seconds sprint on the jump rope
- Plyo: 20r box jumps, then 60 seconds sprint on jump rope
- Plyo: 30r box jumps, 90 seconds sprint on the jump rope
- Rest 1 minute

25-35 minutes

Round 3
- 15 seconds 2-handed KB swing, then15 seconds DB plank row
- 30 seconds 2-handed KB swing, then 30 seconds DB plank row
- 45 seconds 2-handed KB swing, then 45 seconds DB plank row
- Rest for 1 minute

Novice-Advanced

Round 4
- 15 seconds KB side lunges, then 15 seconds pull-ups
- 30 seconds KB side lunges, then 30 seconds pull-ups
- 45 seconds KB side lunges, then 45 seconds pull-ups

SS

Round 5
- 1 minute center splits
- 1 minute front splits
- 1 minute moving through down dogs

Notes and Date

written by Katalin Ogren

MUSCULAR ENDURANCE, PULLING ACTIONS & CORE

Round 1
- 10r alternating lunges with a knee lift
- 10r squats on a bosu
- 10r side planks on the bosu
- 10r alternating leg lifts
- 10r push ups on the bosu

Round 2
- 12-15r face-pulls
- 12r Pop ups
- Repeat for 3 sets

Round 3
- 12-15r seated row
- 20r jack knife sit ups
- Repeat for 3 sets

Round 4
- 12-15r lat pull downs with a wide grip
- 5r single leg squats per leg on bosu
- Repeat for 3 sets

Round 5
- 12-15r cable bicep curls
- 20r knee tucks in plank
- Repeat for 3 sets

Round 6
- 10r arm circles in each direction
- 10r sit and reaches
- Stretch lower back

Notes and Date

Gym Workout

30-35 minutes

Any Level

• *written by Katalin Ogren*

MUSCULAR ENDURANCE, PUSHING ACTIONS, LEGS, CORE

Round 1
- 3 minutes run on treadmill
- 2 minutes leg stretches
- Stretch lower back
- 10r arm circles in each direction
- 30 bicycle crunches

Round 2
- 12-15r step ups with DB
- 12-20r push-ups
- Repeat for 2-3 sets
- 30 cable torso rotations

Round 3
- 12-15r leg press
- 12-15r chest press
- Repeat for 2-3 sets
- 30 bicycle crunches

Round 4
- 12-15r DB side raises
- 30 seconds plank hold
- 12-15r DB shoulder press
- 30 seconds plank hold
- 12-15r DB front raises
- 30 seconds plank hold
- 12-15r DB shoulder press

Round 5
- 2 minutes hamstring stretch on your back
- 1 minute butterfly stretch

Notes and Date

• written by Katalin Ogren

Gym Workout

50-60 minutes

Any Level

FAV

STRENGTH, PULLING ACTION, CORE, STABILITY

Round 1
- 10r air squats with overhead reaches
- 10r alternating lunges
- 10r side lunges with a reach
- 1 minute shadow box

Round 2
- 8-10r DB bent over row
- 30 seconds side plank each side
- 10r push up walking side to side
- 30 seconds single leg balance
- 8-10r pull ups
- Repeat 4 sets

Round 3
- 8-10r DB plank row
- 30 seconds toe dips
- 10r Ys from a prone position
- 8-10r DB bicep curls
- 30 seconds sit up with a DB
- Repeat 4 sets

Round 4
- 5 minutes stretching

Gym Workout

40-50 minutes

Beginner Level

FAV

Notes and Date

• written by Katalin Ogren

STRENGTH, LEGS, STABILITY, CORE

Round 1
- 10r arm circles in each direction
- 10r alternating lunges
- 30r seconds plank
- 10r push ups
- 10r Ts from a prone position
- Hamstring stretches

Round 2
- 6-8r DB or SB squats / HWT
- 30 seconds single balance
- Repeat for 4 sets

Round 3
- 6-8r side lunges with DB / HWT
- 20 supermans
- Repeat for 4 sets

Round 4
- 6-8r DB or SB lunges / HWT
- 30 seconds lateral side steps to a single leg balance
- Repeat for 4 sets

Round 5
- 6-8r hamstring curls
- 6-8r leg extensions
- Repeat for 4 sets

Round 6
- 40r abs, single leg jack knife
- 1 minute hamstring stretch
- 40r side knee tucks in a plank
- Hip stretches

Notes and Date

Gym Workout

40-50 minutes

All Level

• written by Katalin Ogren

POWER, PUSHING ACTIONS, TRICEPS, LEGS, SHOULDERS, CORE

Round 1
- 1 minute shadow box
- 10r air squats with overhead reaches
- 10r alternating lunges
- 10r side lunges with a reach
- 20r crunches on the resist-a-ball

Round 2
- All exercises 20 seconds, with 10 second rest in-between
- Clap pushups
- Squat jumps
- 2 handed KB swing / LWT or MWT
- DB Arnold press
- Repeat for 4 sets

Round 3
- All exercises 20 seconds, with 10 second rest in-between
- KB Turkish get ups each side / LWT or MWT
- Medicine ball chest pass
- Dips
- Hamstring curl jumps
- Repeat for 4 sets

Round 4
- All exercises 20 seconds, with 10 second rest in-between
- DB or SB chest press / LWT or MWT
- DB side lunges / LWT or MWT
- DB side raises / LWT or MWT
- DB tricep overhead press / LWT or MWT
- Repeat for 4 sets

Round 5
- All exercises 20 seconds
- Rotation with medicine ball
- Knee tucks on the ball
- Hip circles
- Bridges on the ball

Notes and Date

Gym Workout

40-50 minutes

Any Level

• *written by Katalin Ogren*

172

TOTAL BODY CONDITIONING

Round 1
- 2 minutes treadmill walk
- 2 minutes treadmill incline walk
- 1 minute treadmill run
- 30 second sprint
- 30 second walk
- 30 seconds sprint
- 30 seconds walk
- 3 minutes stretching

Round 2
- 10-12r step ups with DB alternating legs
- 10-12r any kicks per side
- 10-12r step ups with DB alternating legs
- 10-12r any kicks per side
- 10-20r push ups, any type
- 30 seconds shadow boxing
- 10-20r push ups, any type
- 30 seconds shadow boxing

Round 3
- 10-12r cable abduction lifts, both sides
- Repeat for 3 sets

Round 4
- 10-12 r cable jab, both sides
- Repeat for 3 sets

Round 5
- 10-12r cable knee strikes, both sides
- Repeat for 3 sets

Round 6
- 10-12r cable cross jabs, both sides
- Repeat for 3 sets

• written by Katalin Ogren

Gym Workout

60-65 minutes

Continued

TOTAL BODY CONDITIONING Continued

Round 7
- Plyo: 10-12r sprawl jump tucks, then 30 seconds center splits
- Plyo: 10-12r pop ups, then 15 seconds front splits, both sides
- Plyo: 10-12r box jumps, then 30 seconds sit and reach stretch

Round 8
- 10-12r cable uppercuts, both sides
- Repeat for 3 sets

Round 9
- 30 seconds shadow boxing
- 30 plank hold
- 30 seconds down dog
- 30 bird dogs
- 30 seconds hamstring stretches
- 30 seconds lower back stretch

Notes and Date

• *written by Katalin Ogren*

Gym Workout

60-65 minutes

ADV

SS

FAV

TOTAL BODY MUSCULAR ENDURANCE TRAINING

Round 1
- 1 minutes on the jump rope
- 30 seconds air squats
- 1 minute on the jump rope
- 30 seconds alternating lunges no weight
- 10 minute alternating leg lifts
- 30r arm circles, both sides

Any Setting

Round 2
- 20 seconds 2 handed kettle bell swings, MWT
- 20r push ups then, 20 seconds sprawls, 10 second rest
- 20 seconds, 2 handed kettle bell swings, HWT
- 20r push ups then, 20 seconds sprawls, 10 second rest
- 20 seconds, 2 handed kettle bell swings, HWT
- 20r push ups then, 20 seconds sprawls, 10 second rest

45-50 minutes

Round 3
- 20 seconds DB or KB row, both sides, HWT
- 20 seconds sprint on the jump rope, 10 second rest
- 20 seconds DB or KB row, both sides, HWT
- 20 seconds sprint on the jump rope, 10 second rest
- 20 seconds DB or KB row, both sides, HWT
- 20 seconds sprint on the jump rope, 10 second rest

ADV

Round 4
- 20 seconds KB snatch, both sides, HWT
- 20 KB sit ups, HWT, 10 seconds rest
- 20 seconds KB snatch, both sides, HWT
- 20 KB sit ups, HWT, 10 seconds rest
- 20 seconds KB snatch, both sides, HWT
- 20 KB sit ups, HWT, 10 seconds rest

FAV

Round 5
- 20 seconds turkish get up, both sides, HWT
- 20 seconds side lunges, alternating sides, HWT, 10 seconds rest
- 20 seconds turkish get up, both sides, HWT
- 20 seconds side lunges, alternating sides, HWT, 10 seconds rest
- 20 seconds turkish get up, both sides, HWT
- 20 seconds side lunges, alternating sides, HWT, 10 seconds rest

Round 6
- 3 minutes hamstring stretch
- 2 minutes lower back stretch

Notes and Date

• written by Katalin Ogren

TOTAL BODY CONDITIONING, BODY WEIGHT

Round 1
- 30 seconds jump rope
- 30 seconds plank hold
- 30 seconds back extensions
- 30 seconds pop ups
- 30 seconds air squats
- 30 seconds downdog

Round 2
- 30 seconds each exercise, no rest in-between
- Alternating lunges, weights optional
- Single leg pikes
- Decline push ups
- Plyo: sprawl jump tucks
- 30 seconds rest

Round 3
- 30 seconds each exercise, no rest in-between
- Pull-ups, any style or modification
- Alternating lunges, weight optional
- Plyo: jumping knee tucks
- Dips, any style or modification
- 30 second rest

Round 4
- 30 seconds each exercise, no rest in-between
- Plyo: Hamstring curl jumps
- Pushups, any style or modification
- Bicycle crunches
- Side lunges, alternating sides, weights optional
- 30 seconds rest

Round 5
- 30 seconds each exercise, no rest in-between
- Pull-ups, any style or modification
- Plyo: hamstring curl jumps
- Dips, any style or modification
- 30 seconds rest

Round 6
- 30 seconds each exercise, no rest in-between
- Sprawl jump tucks
- Alternating lunges, weights optional
- Decline push ups
- Single leg pikes
- 30 seconds rest

Any Setting

30 minutes

Any Level

FAV

• *written by Katalin Ogren*

Continued

TOTAL BODY CONDITIONING, BODY WEIGHT, Continued

Round 7

- 30 seconds each exercise, no rest in-between
- Side lunges, alternating sides
- Bicycle crunches
- Pull-ups, any style or modification
- Dips, any style or modification
- 30 second rest

Round 8

- 30 seconds each dynamic flexibility exercise, no rest in-between
- Arm circles alternating sides
- Front leg lift across the body
- Inner thigh leg stretch kicks, alternating sides
- Downdog

Notes and Date

Any Setting

30 minutes

Any Level

FAV

• written by Katalin Ogren

STRENGTH, LEGS, CORE, FLEXIBILITY

Round 1
- 5 minutes bike
- 3 minutes leg lifts in all directions
- 1 minute center split stretch

Round 2
- 8-10r leg press, MWT
- 30 seconds plank hold/30 second rest
- 6-8r leg press, HWT
- 30 seconds plank hold/30-60 second rest
- 4-6r leg press, HWT
- 30 seconds plank hold/30-60 second rest
- 3-5r leg press, HWT
- 30 seconds plank hold/ 1-2 minutes rest
- 3-5r leg press, HWT
- 30 seconds plank hold/1-2 minutes rest
- Hamstring stretch / 2-3 minute rest

Round 3
- 8-10r squat with rack, MWT
- 30 seconds toes dips
- 6-8r squat with rack, HWT
- 30 seconds toes dips
- 4-6r squat with rack, HWT
- 30 seconds toes dips
- 3-5r squat with rack, HWT
- 30 seconds toes dips
- 3-5r squat with rack, HWT
- 30 seconds toes dips
- Lower back stretch

Round 4
- 8-10r hamstring curls, MWT
- 30 seconds Ys or Ts laying on stomach
- 6-8r hamstring curls, HWT
- 30 seconds Ys or Ts laying on stomach
- 4-6r hamstring curls, HWT
- 30 seconds Ys or Ts laying on stomach
- 3-5r hamstring curls HWT
- 30 seconds Ys or Ts laying on stomach
- 3-5r hamstring curls HWT
- 30 seconds Ys or Ts laying on stomach
- Downdog

• *written by Katalin Ogren*

Gym Workout

60-65 minutes

ADV

FAV

Continued

178

STRENGTH, LEGS, CORE, FLEXIBILITY Continued

Round 5

- 8-10r lunges with DB or rack, MWT
- 30 seconds roll-outs on the ball
- 6-8r lunges with DB or rack, HWT
- 30 seconds roll-outs on the ball
- 4-6r lunges with DB or rack, HWT
- 30 seconds bridges off the ball
- 3-5r lunges with DB or rack, HWT
- 30 seconds bridges off the ball
- 3-5r lunges with DB or rack, HWT
- 30 seconds bridges off the ball
- Center splits

Round 6

- 30 seconds right leg hamstring stretch
- 30 seconds left leg hamstring stretch
- 30 seconds butterfly stretch
- 30 seconds lower back stretch
- 30 Downdog

Notes and Date

Gym Workout

60-65 minutes

• *written by Katalin Ogren*

STRENGTH UPPER BODY, PLYOMETRICS

Round 1
- 5 minutes elliptical
- 3 minutes leg lifts in all directions

Round 2
- 8-10r lat pull down, MWT
- Plyo: 30 seconds pop ups / 30-60 second rest
- 6-8r lat pull down, HWT
- Ply: 30 seconds pop ups / 60 second rest
- 4-6r lat pull down, HWT
- Plyo: 30 seconds pop ups / 60-90 second rest
- 3-5r lat pull down, HWT
- Plyo: 30 seconds pop ups / 90-120 second rest
- 3-5r lat pull down, HWT
- Hamstring stretch

Round 3
- 8-10r chest press or fly, MWT
- Plyo: 30 seconds hamstring curl jumps / 30-60 second rest
- 6-8r chest press or fly, HWT
- Plyo: 30 seconds hamstring curl jumps / 60 second rest
- 4-6r chest press or fly, HWT
- Plyo: 30 seconds hamstring curl jumps / 60-90 second rest
- 3-5r chest press or fly, HWT
- Plyo: 30 seconds hamstring curl jumps / 90-120 second rest
- 3-5r chest press or fly, HWT
- Lower back stretch

Round 4
- 8-10r DB bent over row, MWT
- 30 seconds jump rope / 30-60 second rest
- 6-8r DB bent over row, HWT
- 30 seconds jump rope / 60 second rest
- 4-6r DB bent over row, HWT
- 30 seconds jump rope / 60-90 second rest
- 3-5r DB bent over row, HWT
- 30 seconds jump rope / 90-120 second rest
- 3-5r DB bent over row, HWT
- Arm circles

- *written by Katalin Ogren*

Gym Workout

60-70 minutes

Continued

STRENGTH UPPER BODY, PLYOMETRICS Continued

Round 5

- 8-10r DB side raise, MWT
- 30 seconds single leg pikes / 30-60 second rest
- 6-8r DB side raise, HWT
- 30 seconds single leg pikes / 60 second rest
- 4-6r DB side raise, HWT
- 30 seconds single leg pikes / 60-90 second rest
- 3-5r DB side raise, HWT
- 30 seconds single leg pikes / 90-120 second rest
- 3-5r DB side raise, HWT
- 10r arm circles, al directions, both sides

Round 6

- 8-10r DB side raise, MWT
- 30 seconds single leg pikes / 30-60 second rest
- 6-8r DB side raise, HWT
- 30 seconds single leg pikes / 60 second rest
- 4-6r DB side raise, HWT
- 30 seconds single leg pikes / 60-90 second rest
- 3-5r DB side raise, HWT
- 30 seconds single leg pikes / 90-120 second rest
- 3-5r DB side raise, HWT
- 10r arm circles, all directions, both sides

Round 7

- Max out on reps (Hypertrophy round)
- Pull-ups, any style
- Pushups, any style
- Repeat 4 sets

Notes and Date

Gym Workout

60-70 minutes

ADV

FAV

- *written by Katalin Ogren*

UPPER BODY MUSCULAR ENDURANCE

Round 1
- 30 seconds arm circle
- 30 seconds pushups
- 30 seconds bird dogs
- 30 seconds Ys on stomach
- 30 seconds Ts on stomach
- 15-20r cable rotator cuff both sides, both directions

Round 2
- 12-15r cable high chop from lunge, both sides
- Repeat for 3 sets

Round 3
- 12-15r cable standing chest fly, both sides
- Repeat for 3 sets

Round 4
- 12-15r cable wide row alternating sides
- 12-15r DB plank row
- Repeat for 3 sets

Round 5
- 12-15r cable cross jabs, both sides
- Repeat for 3 sets

Round 6
- 12-15r cable standing lateral flexion, both sides
- 12-15r cable straight arm overhead row
- Repeat for 3 sets
- 30 seconds Ys on stomach

Round 7
- 12-15r cable bicep curls
- 12-15r cable tricep press downs
- Repeat for 3 sets
- 30 seconds Ts on stomach
- 12-15r arm circles, both sides, both directions

Notes and Date

Gym Workout

45-50 minutes

Any Level

SS

• *written by Katalin Ogren*

TOTAL BODY STRENGTH

Round 1
- 12-20r decline push ups
- 10r arm circles, both arms, both directions
- 20r air squats
- Hamstring stretches
- 10r pelvic bridges

Round 2
- 6-8r chest press with SB, HWT
- 10r single leg squats with ground touches
- 6r pull-ups, add band for assistance or weight for challenge
- Repeat x 4 increase weight for challenge

Round 3
- 6-8r leg press or split squat, HWT
- 10r walking push ups moving side to side
- 6-8r lat pull down, HWT
- Repeat x 4 increase weight for challenge

Round 4
- 6-8r arnold press, HWT
- 30r any abs
- 6-8r plank row with DB, HWT,
- Repeat x 4 increase weight for challenge

Round 5
- 20r alternating leg lifts
- Total body static stretches

Notes and Date

Gym Workout

45-50 minutes

Great for Beginners

- *written by Katalin Ogren*

183

STRENGTH, POWER, LEGS

Round 1
- 1 minute on the jump rope
- 30 seconds air squats
- 1 minute on the jump rope
- 30 seconds alternating lunges no weight
- 10r alternating leg lifts
- 30r arm circles, both sides
- 30 seconds plank hold
- 30r squat jumps
- 30 seconds bird dogs

Round 2
- 20 seconds for each exercise, 10 seconds rest in-between
- KB swing 1 or 2 handed, HWT
- High knee run in place or sprint on jump rope
- Plyo: Sprawl jump knee tucks
- Squats with DB, HWT
- Repeat for 4 sets
- Rest 1-2 minutes

Round 3
- 20 seconds for each exercise, 10 seconds rest in-between
- Right leg lunge/split squat with DB, HWT
- Left leg lunge/split squat with DB, HWT
- Plyo: Hamstring curl jumps
- Plank with side knees alternating sides quickly
- Repeat for 4 sets
- Rest 1-2 minutes

Round 4
- 20 seconds for each exercise, 10 seconds rest in-between
- KB snatch and press right arm
- KB snatch and press left arm
- Plyo: Box jumps
- KB side lunges, alternating sides
- Repeat for 4 sets
- Rest 1-2 minutes

Round 5
- 1 minute miscellaneous kicks then, 1 minute downdog
- 1 minute butterfly stretch then, 1 minute center splits
- 1 minute hamstring stretch on each leg

Notes and Date

• written by Katalin Ogren

Any Setting

35 minutes

ADV

TOTAL BODY CIRCUIT

Round 1
- 30 seconds jumping jacks
- 30 seconds air squats
- 30 seconds on the jump rope
- 30 arm circles, both sides
- 30 seconds sit and reach
- 30 seconds rotating upper body, standing twists

Round 2
- Each exercise for 1 minute, no rest in-between
- Jump Rope
- Push ups
- Plyo: Jump squats
- Walking lunges
- Side lunges
- Decline push ups
- Push up, arm reach
- Step ups
- Any Kicks

Round 3
- Each exercise for 1 minute, no rest in-between
- Pull ups
- Plyo: Box jumps
- Right leg split squat
- Left leg split squat
- Clap push ups
- Plyo: Pop ups
- Dips
- Balancing V sits
- Back extension with rotation
- Plyo: Sprawl jump knee tucks

Round 4
- Each exercise for 1 minute, no rest in-between
- Hamstring curls on resist-a-ball
- Wide squats
- Decline push ups
- Dips
- Jump rope
- Ground getups, alternating sides (like turkish get up)
- Pull ups
- Shadow boxing
- Side lunges
- Alternating leg lifts

Notes and Date

Any Setting

45-50 minutes

Any Level

FAV

• written by Katalin Ogren

WRITE YOUR OWN PROGRAM

Round 1

Round 2

Round 3

Round 4

Round 5

Notes, Date

Gym Workout

minutes

Any Level

• written by _____

AUTHOR BIO

KATALIN RODRIGUEZ OGREN

Katalin is the Owner of POW! Mixed Martial Arts and Fitness (www.powkickboxing.com), a certified WBE company. POW! MMA & Fitness has been training Chicagoans since 2001. It has also become the home of POW! Kids (www.POWKidsChicago.com) and POW! Health and Wellness (www.POWHealthandWellness.com). Katalin was the first to bring Krav Maga to Chicago in 2002. Since opening POW! she has exposed her students to a wide range of martial arts including boxing, muay thai, kung fu, jeet kun do, MMA, brazilian jiu jitsu, judo, tai chi, tae kwon do and kickboxing. POW! MMA & Fitness has always been recognized for their quality of technical instruction, fitness programming and integrated cross-training.

Katalin holds 4 black belts and is a certified trainer. She began the martial arts at 9 years old. Her wide exposure to so many martial arts and combat sports has afforded her several writing and speaking engagements since she began her professional career in 1993. With over 30+ years in the martial arts and 20+ years in the fitness industry, she has developed a pedigree that represents accomplishments in both the martial arts and fitness industry. Some of her career highlights include: starred in 17 DVDS, completed a 100-city speaking tour across America, authored 4 industry educational manuals, served as Education Director for Revgear Sports, published over 200 articles in national magazines and played the role of Kitana, Meleena and Jade in the video game *Mortal Kombat 2.*

With Special Thanks to Bernie Lecocq

Bernie is the Owner of Rivernorth Gym (RNG) in Chicago's famous Merchandise Mart. Before opening RNG in 2010, he owned and operated Exercise Endeavors, a boutique fitness center in Chicago's Gold Coast for 7 years. Bernie has over 35,000 hours of experience in personal training. He began his career with B.S. in Corporate Fitness. Today, is operates his corporate fitness center RNG and works actively as a presenter and consultant specializing in wellness, movement biomechanics and program design.

http://www.rivernorthgym.com/

BIBLIOGRAPHY

References

- Aaberg, Everett. Muscle Mechanics (2nd ed). Library of Congress, 2006.
- AAFA. Fitness: Theory & Practice A Comprehensive Resource for Group Fitness Resources (5th ed), 2010.
- Atler, Michael J. Science of Flexibility (3rd ed.) , 2004.
- Bompa, Tudor O and Haff, Gregory, G. Periodization Theory and Methodology of Training (5th ed), 2009.
- Bompa, Tudor O. and Carrera, Michael, C. Periodization Training for Sports, Human Kinetics, 2009.
- Cook, Gray. Athletic Body in Balance, Human Kinetics, 2003.
- Delavier, Frederic. Strength Training Anatomy (3rd ed). Library of Congress,2010.
- Earle, W. Roger and Baechle, R. Thomas. NSCA's Essentials of Personal Training, Hong Kong. 2004.
- Knudson, Duane. Fundamentals of Biomechanics. Library of Congress, 2007.
- Lephart, Scott M. and Fu, Freddie H. Proprioception & Neuromuscular Control in Joint Stability, Library of Congress, 2000.
- O'Brien, Teri S. The Personal Trainers Handbook, Human Kinetics, 2007.
- Siff, M.C., and Y.V. Verkhoshansky.1999. Supertraining. 4th ed. Denver, Colorado: Supertraining International
- Shinkle J, Nesser TW, Demchak TJ, McMannus DM. Effects of Core Strength on the Measure of Power in the Extremities. Journal of Strength & Conditioning Res. 26(2):373-379, 2012.
- Waehner, Paige. "The Most Effective Strength Training Exercises," Health's Disease and Condition. November 15, 2011.

Internet Resources:

- http://sportsmedicine.about.com
- http://exercise.about.com
- http://www.sport-fitness-advisor.com/energysystems.html
- http://www.acefitness.org
- http://www.flammerouge.je/factsheets/methods.htm
- http://www.mayoclinic.org/
- http://www.ptonthenet.com/
- http://www.testerone.com/
- http://www.mikemahler.com/
- www.cdc.gov
- www.nsca.com
- www.ericcressey.com/
- www.precisionnutrition.com
- http://www.T-Nation.com
  http://www.EliteFTS.com

Other Resources

- River North Gym, 222 Merchandise Mart, Chicago, Illinois, 60654 – (www.rivernorthgym.com)
- POW! Mixed Martial Arts and Fitness, 950 W Washington, Chicago, Illinois 60607 (www.powkickboxing.com)